Coping
with
Crisis

Coping with Crisis

James Allen

MEDIA

Published 2020 by Gildan Media LLC
aka G&D Media
www.GandDmedia.com

Front Cover design by David Rheinhardt of Pyrographx

Interior design by Meghan Day Healey of Story Horse, LLC

Library of Congress Cataloging-in-Publication Data is available
upon request

ISBN: 978-1-7225-0351-2

10   9   8   7   6   5   4   3   2   1

Contents

As a Man Thinketh

Mind is the Master power that moulds and makes,

    And Man is Mind, and evermore he takes

The tool of Thought, and, shaping what he wills,

Brings forth a thousand joys, a thousand ills:

    He thinks in secret and it comes to pass:

    Environment is but his looking-glass.

Contents

Foreword

This little volume (the result of meditation and experience) is not intended as an exhaustive treatise on the much-written-upon subject of the power of thought. It is suggestive rather than explanatory, its object being to stimulate men and women to the discovery and perception of the truth that—

They themselves are makers of themselves

by virtue of the thoughts which they choose and encourage; that mind is the master weaver, both of the inner garment of character and the outer garment of circumstance, and that, as they may have hitherto woven in ignorance and pain they may now weave in enlightenment and happiness.

—James Allen

Broad Park Avenue, Ilfracombe, England

Thought and Character

The aphorism "As a man thinketh in his heart so is he" not only embraces the whole of a man's being, but is so comprehensive as to reach out to every condition and circumstance of his life. A man is literally *what he thinks*, his character being the complete sum of all his thoughts.

As the plant springs from, and could not be without, the seed, so every act of a man springs from the hidden seeds of thought, and could not have appeared without them. This applies equally to those acts called "spontaneous" and "unpremeditated" as to those which are deliberately executed.

Act is the blossom of thought, and joy and suffering are its fruits; thus does a man garner in the sweet and bitter fruitage of his own husbandry.

Thought in the mind hath made us. What we are
By thought was wrought and built. If a man's mind
Hath evil thoughts, pain comes on him as comes
The wheel the ox behind. . . .

*   . . . If one endure*
In purity of thought, joy follows him
As his own shadow—sure.

Man is a growth by law, and not a creation by artifice, and cause and effect is as absolute and undeviating in the hidden realm of thought as in the world of visible and material things. A noble and Godlike character is not a thing of favor or chance, but is the natural result of continued effort in right thinking, the effect of long-cherished association with Godlike thoughts. An ignoble and bestial character, by the same process, is the result of the continued harboring of groveling thoughts.

Man is made or unmade by himself; in the armory of thought he forges the weapons by which he destroys himself; he also fashions the tools with which he builds for himself heavenly mansions of joy and strength and peace. By the right choice and true application of thought, man ascends to the Divine Perfection; by the abuse and wrong application of thought, he descends below the level of the beast. Between these two extremes are all the grades of character, and man is their maker and master.

Of all the beautiful truths pertaining to the soul which have been restored and brought to light in this age, none is more gladdening or fruitful of divine promise and confidence than this—that man is the master of thought, the molder of character, and the maker and shaper of condition, environment, and destiny.

As a being of Power, Intelligence, and Love, and the lord of his own thoughts, man holds the key to every situation, and contains within himself that transforming and regenerative agency by which he may make himself what he wills.

Man is always the master, even in his weakest and most abandoned state; but in his weakness and degradation he is the foolish master who misgoverns his "household." When he begins to reflect upon his condition, and to search diligently for the Law upon which his being is established, he then becomes the wise master, directing his energies with intelligence, and fashioning his thoughts to fruitful issues. Such is the *conscious* master, and man can only thus become by discovering *within himself the* laws of thought; which discovery is totally a matter of application, self-analysis, and experience.

Only by much searching and mining are gold and diamonds obtained, and man can find every truth connected with his being if he will dig deep into the mine of his soul; and that he is the maker of his character, the molder of his life, and the builder of his destiny, he may unerringly prove, if he will watch, control, and alter his thoughts, tracing their effects upon himself, upon others, and upon his life and circumstances, linking cause and effect by patient practice and investigation, and utilizing his every experience, even to the most trivial, everyday occurrence, as a means of obtaining that knowledge of himself which is Understanding, Wisdom, Power. In this direction, as in no other, is the law absolute that "He that seeketh findeth; and to him that knocketh it shall be opened"; for only by patience, practice, and ceaseless importunity can a man enter the Door of the Temple of Knowledge.

Effect of Thought on Circumstances

A man's mind may be likened to a garden, which may be intelligently cultivated or allowed to run wild; but whether cultivated or neglected, it must, and will, *bring forth*. If no useful seeds are *put* into it, then an abundance of useless weed seeds will *fall* therein, and will continue to produce their kind.

Just as a gardener cultivates his plot, keeping it free from weeds, and growing the flowers and fruits which he requires, so may a man tend the garden of his mind, weeding out all the wrong, useless, and impure thoughts, and cultivating toward perfection the flowers and fruits of right, useful, and pure thoughts. By pursuing this process, a man sooner or later discovers that he is the master gardener of his soul, the director of his life. He also reveals, within himself, the laws of thought, and understands, with ever-increasing accuracy, how the thought forces and mind elements operate in the shaping of his character, circumstances, and destiny.

Thought and character are one, and as character can only manifest and discover itself through environment and circumstance, the outer conditions of a person's life will always be found to be harmoniously related to his inner state. This does not mean that a man's circumstances at any given time are an indication of his *entire* character, but that those circumstances are so intimately connected with some vital thought element within himself that, for the time being, they are indispensable to his development.

Every man is where he is by the law of his being; the thoughts which he has built into his character have brought him there, and in the arrangement of his life there is no element of chance, but all is the result of a law which cannot err. This is just as true of those who feel "out of harmony" with their surroundings as of those who are contented with them.

As a progressive and evolving being, man is where he is that he may learn that he may grow; and as he learns the spiritual lesson which any circumstance contains for him, it passes away and gives place to other circumstances.

Man is buffeted by circumstances so long as he believes himself to be the creature of outside conditions, but when he realizes that he is a creative power, and that he may command the hidden soil and seeds of his being out of which circumstances grow, he then becomes the rightful master of himself.

That circumstances *grow* out of thought every man knows who has for any length of time practiced self-control and self-purification, for he will have noticed that the alteration in his circumstances has been in exact ratio with his altered mental condition. So true is this that when a man earnestly applies himself to remedy the defects in his character, and makes swift and marked progress, he passes rapidly through a succession of vicissitudes.

The soul attracts that which it secretly harbors; that which it loves, and also that which it fears; it reaches the height of its cherished aspirations; it falls to the level of its unchastened desires—and circumstances are the means by which the soul receives its own.

Every thought seed sown or allowed to fall into the mind, and to take root there, produces its own, blossoming sooner or later into act, and bearing its own fruitage of opportunity and circumstance. Good thoughts bear good fruit, bad thoughts bad fruit.

The outer world of circumstance shapes itself to the inner world of thought, and both pleasant and unpleasant external conditions are factors which make for the ultimate good of the individual. As the reaper of his own harvest, man learns both by suffering and bliss.

Following the inmost desires, aspirations, thoughts, by which he allows himself to be dominated (pursuing the will-o'-the-wisps of impure imaginings or steadfastly walking the highway of strong and high endeavor), a man at last arrives at their fruition and fulfillment in the outer conditions of his life. The laws of growth and adjustment everywhere obtain.

A man does not come to the almshouse or the jail by the tyranny of fate or circumstance, but by the pathway of groveling thoughts and base desires. Nor does a pure-minded man fall suddenly into crime by stress of any mere external force; the criminal thought had long been secretly fostered in the heart, and the hour of opportunity revealed its gathered power. Circumstance does not make the man; it reveals him to himself. No such conditions can exist as descending into vice and its attendant sufferings apart from vicious inclinations, or ascending into virtue and its pure happiness without the continued cultivation of virtuous aspirations; and man, therefore, as the lord and master of thought, is the maker of himself, the shaper and author of environment. Even at birth the soul comes to its own, and through every step of its earthly pilgrimage it attracts those combinations of conditions which reveal itself, which are the reflections of its own purity and impurity, its strength and weakness.

Men do not attract that which they *want*, but that which they *are*. Their whims, fancies, and ambitions are thwarted at every step, but their inmost thoughts and desires are fed with their own food, be it foul or clean. The "divinity that shapes our ends" is in ourselves; it is our very self. Man is manacled only by himself: thought and action are the jailers of Fate—they imprison, being base; they are also the angels of Freedom—they liberate, being noble. Not what he wishes and prays for does a man get, but what he justly earns. His wishes and prayers are only gratified and answered when they harmonize with his thoughts and actions.

In the light of this truth, what, then, is the meaning of "fighting against circumstances"? It means that a man is continually revolting against an *effect* without, while all the time he is nourishing and preserving its *cause* in his heart. That cause may take the form of a conscious vice or an unconscious weakness; but whatever it is, it stubbornly retards the efforts of its possessor, and thus calls aloud for remedy.

Men are anxious to improve their circumstances, but are unwilling to improve themselves; they therefore remain bound. The man who does not shrink from self-crucifixion can never fail to accomplish the object upon which his heart is set. This is as true of earthly as of heavenly things. Even the man whose sole object is to acquire wealth must be prepared to make great personal sacrifices before he can accomplish his object; and how much more so he who would realize a strong and well-poised life?

Here is a man who is wretchedly poor. He is extremely anxious that his surroundings and home comforts should be improved, yet all the time he shirks his work, and considers he is justified in trying to deceive his employer on the ground of the insufficiency of his wages. Such a man does not understand the simplest rudiments of those principles which are the basis of true prosperity, and is not only totally unfitted to rise out of his wretchedness, but is actually attracting to himself a still deeper wretchedness by dwelling in, and acting out, indolent, deceptive, and unmanly thoughts.

Here is a rich man who is the victim of a painful and persistent disease as the result of gluttony. He is willing to give large sums of money to get rid of it, but he will not sacrifice his gluttonous desires.

He wants to gratify his taste for rich and unnatural viands and have his health as well. Such a man is totally unfit to have health, because he has not yet learned the first principles of a healthy life.

Here is an employer of labor who adopts crooked measures to avoid paying the regulation wage, and, in the hope of making larger profits, reduces the wages of his workpeople. Such a man is altogether unfitted for prosperity, and when he finds himself bankrupt, both as regards reputation and riches, he blames circumstances, not knowing that he is the sole author of his condition.

I have introduced these three cases merely as illustrative of the truth that man is the causer (though nearly always unconsciously) of his circumstances, and that, while aiming at a good end, he is continually frustrating its accomplishment by encouraging thoughts and desires which cannot possibly harmonize with that end. Such cases could be multiplied and varied almost indefinitely, but this is not necessary, as the reader can, if he so resolves, trace the action of the laws of thought in his own mind and life, and until this is done, mere external facts cannot serve as a ground of reasoning.

Circumstances, however, are so complicated, thought is so deeply rooted, and the conditions of happiness vary so vastly with individuals that a man's *entire* soul condition (although it may be known to himself) cannot be judged by another from the external aspect of his life alone. A man may be honest in certain directions, yet suffer privations; a man may be dishonest in certain directions, yet acquire wealth; but the conclusion usually formed that the one man fails *because of his particular honesty*, and that the other prospers *because of his particular dishonesty*, is the result of a superficial judgment, which assumes that the dishonest man is almost totally corrupt, and the honest man almost entirely virtuous. In the light of a deeper knowledge and wider experience, such judgment is found to be erroneous. The dishonest man may have some admirable virtues which the other does not possess; and the honest man obnoxious vices which are absent in the other. The honest man reaps the good results of his honest thoughts and acts; he also brings upon himself the sufferings which his vices produce. The dishonest man likewise garners his own suffering and happiness.

It is pleasing to human vanity to believe that one suffers because of one's virtue; but not until a man has extirpated every sickly, bitter, and impure thought from his mind, and washed every sinful stain from his soul, can he be in a position to know and declare that his sufferings are the result of his good, and not of his bad qualities; and on the way to, yet long before he has reached, that supreme perfection, he will have found, working in his mind and life, the Great Law which is absolutely just, and which cannot, therefore, give good for evil, evil for good. Possessed of such knowledge, he will then know, looking back upon his past ignorance and blindness, that his life is, and always was, justly ordered, and that all his past experiences, good and bad, were the equitable outworking of his evolving, yet unevolved self.

Good thoughts and actions can never produce bad results; bad thoughts and actions can never produce good results. This is but saying that nothing can come from corn but corn, nothing from nettles but nettles. Men understand this law in the natural world, and work with it; but few understand it in the mental and moral world (though its operation there is just as simple and undeviating), and they, therefore, do not cooperate with it.

Suffering is *always* the effect of wrong thought in some direction. It is an indication that the individual is out of harmony with himself, with the Law of his being. The sole and supreme use of suffering is to purify, to burn out all that is useless and impure. Suffering ceases for him who is pure. There could be no object in burning gold after the dross had been removed, and a perfectly pure and enlightened being could not suffer.

The circumstances which a man encounters with suffering are the result of his own mental inharmony. The circumstances which a man encounters with blessedness are the result of his own mental harmony. Blessedness, not material possessions, is the measure of right thought; wretchedness, not lack of material possessions, is the measure of wrong thought. A man may be cursed and rich; he may be blessed and poor. Blessedness and riches are only joined together when the riches are rightly and wisely used; and the poor man only descends into wretchedness when he regards his lot as a burden unjustly imposed.

Indigence and indulgence are the two extremes of wretchedness. They are both equally unnatural and the result of mental disorder. A man is not rightly conditioned until he is a happy, healthy, and prosperous being; and happiness, health, and prosperity are the result of a harmonious adjustment of the inner with the outer, of the man with his surroundings.

A man only begins to be a man when he ceases to whine and revile, and commences to search for the hidden justice which regulates his life. And as he adapts his mind to that regulating factor, he ceases to accuse others as the cause of his condition, and builds himself up in strong and noble thoughts; ceases to kick against circumstances, but begins to use them as aids to his more rapid progress, and as a means of discovering the hidden powers and possibilities within himself.

Law, not confusion, is the dominating principle in the universe; justice, not injustice, is the soul and substance of life; and righteousness, not corruption, is the molding and moving force in the spiritual government of the world. This being so, man has but to right himself to find that the universe is right; and during the process of putting himself right, he will find that as he alters his thoughts toward things, and other people, things and other people will alter toward him.

The proof of this truth is in every person, and it therefore admits of easy investigation by systematic introspection and self-analysis. Let a man radically alter his thoughts, and he will be astonished at the rapid transformation it will effect in the material conditions of his life. Men imagine that thought can be kept secret, but it cannot; it rapidly crystallizes into habit, and habit solidifies into circumstance. Bestial thoughts crystallize into habits of drunkenness and sensuality, which solidify into circumstances of destitution and disease; impure thoughts of every kind crystallize into enervating and confusing habits, which solidify into distracting and adverse circumstances; thoughts of fear, doubt, and indecision crystallize into weak, unmanly, and irresolute habits, which solidify into circumstances of failure, indigence, and slavish dependence; lazy thoughts crystallize into habits of uncleanliness and dishonesty, which solidify into circumstances of foulness and beggary; hateful and condemnatory thoughts crystallize into habits of accusation and violence, which solidify into circumstances of injury and persecution; selfish thoughts of all kinds crystallize into habits of self-seeking, which solidify into circumstances more or less distressing. On the other hand, beautiful thoughts of all kinds crystallize into habits of grace and kindliness, which solidify into genial and sunny circumstances; pure thoughts crystallize into habits of temperance and self-control, which solidify into circumstances of repose and peace; thoughts of courage, self-reliance, and decision crystallize into manly habits, which solidify into circumstances of success, plenty, and freedom; energetic thoughts crystallize into habits of cleanliness and industry, which solidify into circumstances of pleasantness; gentle and forgiving thoughts crystallize into habits of gentleness, which solidify into protective and preservative circumstances; loving and unselfish thoughts crystallize into habits of self-forgetfulness for others, which solidify into circumstances of sure and abiding prosperity and true riches.

A particular train of thought persisted in, be it good or bad, cannot fail to produce its results on the character and circumstances. A man cannot *directly* choose his circumstances, but he can choose his thoughts, and so indirectly, yet surely, shape his circumstances.

Nature helps every man to the gratification of the thoughts which he most encourages, and opportunities are presented which will most speedily bring to the surface both the good and evil thoughts.

Let a man cease from his sinful thoughts, and all the world will soften toward him, and be ready to help him; let him put away his weakly and sickly thoughts, and lo! opportunities will spring up on every hand to aid his strong resolves; let him encourage good thoughts, and no hard fate shall bind him down to wretchedness and shame. The world is your kaleidoscope, and the varying combinations of colors which at every succeeding moment it presents to you are the exquisitely adjusted pictures of your ever-moving thoughts.

You will be what you will to be;
Let failure find its false content
In that poor word, "environment,"
But spirit scorns it, and is free.

It masters time, it conquers space;
It cows that boastful trickster, Chance,
And bids the tyrant Circumstance
Uncrown, and fill a servant's place.

The human Will, that force unseen,
The offspring of a deathless Soul,
Can hew a way to any goal,
Though walls of granite intervene.

Be not impatient in delay,
But wait as one who understands;
When spirit rises and commands,
The gods are ready to obey.

Effect of Thought on Health and the Body

The body is the servant of the mind. It obeys the operations of the mind, whether they be deliberately chosen or automatically expressed. At the bidding of unlawful thoughts the body sinks rapidly into disease and decay; at the command of glad and beautiful thoughts it becomes clothed with youthfulness and beauty.

Disease and health, like circumstances, are rooted in thought. Sickly thoughts will express themselves through a sickly body. Thoughts of fear have been known to kill a man as speedily as a bullet, and they are continually killing thousands of people just as surely though less rapidly. The people who live in fear of disease are the people who get it. Anxiety quickly demoralizes the whole body, and lays it open to the entrance of disease; while impure thoughts, even if not physically indulged, will soon shatter the nervous system.

Strong, pure, and happy thoughts build up the body in vigor and grace. The body is a delicate and plastic instrument, which responds readily to the thoughts by which it is impressed, and habits of thought will produce their own effects, good or bad, upon it.

Men will continue to have impure and poisoned blood so long as they propagate unclean thoughts. Out of a clean heart comes a clean life and a clean body. Out of a defiled mind proceeds a defiled life and a corrupt body. Thought is the font of action, life, and manifestation; make the fountain pure, and all will be pure.

Change of diet will not help a man who will not change his thoughts. When a man makes his thoughts pure, he no longer desires impure food.

Clean thoughts make clean habits. The so-called saint who does not wash his body is not a saint. He who has strengthened and purified his thoughts does not need to consider the malevolent microbe.

If you would perfect your body, guard your mind. If you would renew your body, beautify your mind. Thoughts of malice, envy, disappointment, despondency rob the body of its health and grace. A sour face does not come by chance; it is made by sour thoughts. Wrinkles that mar are drawn by folly, passion, pride.

I know a woman of ninety-six who has the bright, innocent face of a girl. I know a man well under middle age whose face is drawn into inharmonious contours. The one is the result of a sweet and sunny disposition; the other is the outcome of passion and discontent.

As you cannot have a sweet and wholesome abode unless you admit the air and sunshine freely into your rooms, so a strong body and a bright, happy, or serene countenance can only result from the free admittance into the mind of thoughts of joy and good will and serenity.

On the faces of the aged there are wrinkles made by sympathy; others by strong and pure thought; and others are carved by passion: who cannot distinguish them? With those who have lived righteously, age is calm, peaceful, and softly mellowed, like the setting sun. I have recently seen a philosopher on his deathbed. He was not old except in years. He died as sweetly and peacefully as he had lived.

There is no physician like cheerful thought for dissipating the ills of the body; there is no com-

forter to compare with good will for dispersing
the shadows of grief and sorrow. To live continually in thoughts of ill will, cynicism, suspicion, and
envy is to be Confined in a self-made prison hole.
But to think well of all, to be cheerful with all, to
patiently learn to find the good in all—such unselfish thoughts are the very portals of heaven; and
to dwell day by day in thoughts of peace toward
every creature will bring abounding peace to their
possessor.

Thought
and Purpose

Until thought is linked with purpose there is no intelligent accomplishment. With the majority the bark of thought is allowed to "drift" upon the ocean of life. Aimlessness is a vice, and such drifting must not continue for him who would steer clear of catastrophe and destruction.

They who have no central purpose in their life fall an easy prey to petty worries, fears, troubles, and self-pityings, all of which are indications of weakness, which lead, just as surely as deliberately planned sins (though by a different route), to failure, unhappiness, and loss, for weakness cannot persist in a power-evolving universe.

A man should conceive of a legitimate purpose in his heart, and set out to accomplish it. He should make this purpose the centralizing point of his thoughts. It may take the form of a spiritual ideal, or it may be a worldly object, according to his nature at the time being; but whichever it is, he should steadily focus his thought forces upon the object which he has set before him. He should make this purpose his supreme duty, and should devote himself to its attainment, not allowing his thoughts to wander away into ephemeral fancies, longings, and imaginings. This is the royal road to self-control and true concentration of thought. Even if he fails again and again to accomplish his purpose (as he necessarily must until weakness is overcome), the *strength of character gained* will be the measure of his *true* success, and this will form a new starting point for future power and triumph.

Those who are not prepared for the apprehension of a *great* purpose should fix their thoughts upon the faultless performance of their duty, no matter how insignificant their task may appear. Only in this way can the thoughts be gathered and focused, and resolution and energy be developed, which being done, there is nothing which may not be accomplished.

The weakest soul, knowing its own weakness, and believing this truth—*that strength can only be developed by effort and practice*—will, thus believing, at once begin to exert itself, and, adding effort to effort, patience to patience, and strength to strength, will never cease to develop, and will at last grow divinely strong.

As the physically weak man can make himself strong by careful and patient training, so the man of weak thoughts can make them strong by exercising himself in right thinking.

To put away aimlessness and weakness, and to begin to think with purpose, is to enter the ranks of those strong ones who only recognize failure as one of the pathways to attainment; who make all conditions serve them, and who think strongly, attempt fearlessly, and accomplish masterfully.

Having conceived of his purpose, a man should mentally mark out a *straight* pathway to its achievement, looking neither to the right nor the left. Doubts and fears should be rigorously excluded; they are disintegrating elements which break up the straight line of effort, rendering it crooked, ineffectual, useless. Thoughts of doubt and fear never accomplish anything, and never can. They always lead to failure. Purpose, energy, power to do, and all strong thoughts cease when doubt and fear creep in.

The will to do springs from the knowledge that we *can* do. Doubt and fear are the great enemies of knowledge, and he who encourages them, who does not slay them, thwarts himself at every step.

He who has conquered doubt and fear has conquered failure. His every thought is allied with power, and all difficulties are bravely met and wisely overcome. His purposes are seasonably planted, and they bloom and bring forth fruit which does not fall prematurely to the ground.

Thought allied fearlessly to purpose becomes creative force: he who *knows* this is ready to become something higher and stronger than a mere bundle of wavering thoughts and fluctuating sensations; he who does this has become the conscious and intelligent wielder of his mental powers.

The Thought-Factor In Achievement

All that a man achieves and all that he fails to achieve is the direct result of his own thoughts. In a justly ordered universe, where loss of equipoise would mean total destruction, individual responsibility must be absolute. A man's weakness and strength, purity and impurity, are his own, and not another man's; they are brought about by himself, and not by another; and they can only be altered by himself, never by another. His condition is also his own, and not another man's. His suffering and his happiness are evolved from within. As he thinks, so he is; as he continues to think, so he remains.

A strong man cannot help a weaker unless that weaker is *willing* to be helped, and even then the weak man must become strong of himself; he must, by his own efforts, develop the strength which he admires in another. None but himself can alter his condition.

It has been usual for men to think and to say, "Many men are slaves because one is an oppressor; let us hate the oppressor." Now, however, there is among an increasing few a tendency to reverse this judgment, and to say, "One man is an oppressor because many are slaves; let us despise the slaves." The truth is that oppressor and slave are cooperators in ignorance, and, while seeming to afflict each other, are in reality afflicting themselves. A perfect Knowledge perceives the action of law in the weakness of the oppressed and the misapplied power of the oppressor; a perfect Love, seeing the suffering which both states entail, condemns neither; a perfect Compassion embraces both oppressor and oppressed.

He who has conquered weakness, and has put away all selfish thoughts, belongs neither to oppressor nor oppressed. He is free.

A man can only rise, conquer, and achieve by lifting up his thoughts. He can only remain weak, abject, and miserable by refusing to lift up his thoughts.

Before a man can achieve anything, even in worldly things, he must lift his thoughts above slavish animal indulgence. He may not, in order to succeed, give up *all* animality and selfishness, by any means; but a portion of it must, at least, be sacrificed. A man whose first thought is bestial indulgence could neither think clearly nor plan methodically; he could not find and develop his latent resources, and would fail in any undertaking. Not having commenced manfully to control his thoughts, he is not in a position to control affairs and to adopt serious responsibilities. He is not fit to act independently and stand alone. But he is limited only by the thoughts which he chooses.

There can be no progress, no achievement without sacrifice, and a man's worldly success will be in the measure that he sacrifices his confused animal thoughts, and fixes his mind on the development of his plans, and the strengthening of his resolution and self-reliance. And the higher he lifts his thoughts, the more manly, upright, and righteous he becomes, the greater will be his success, the more blessed and enduring will be his achievements.

The universe does not favor the greedy, the dishonest, the vicious, although on the mere surface it may sometimes appear to do so; it helps the honest, the magnanimous, the virtuous. All the great

Teachers of the ages have declared this in varying forms, and to prove and know it a man has but to persist in making himself more and more virtuous by lifting up his thoughts.

Intellectual achievements are the result of thought consecrated to the search for knowledge, or for the beautiful and true in life and nature. Such achievements may be sometimes connected with vanity and ambition, but they are not the outcome of those characteristics; they are the natural outgrowth of long and arduous effort, and of pure and unselfish thoughts.

Spiritual achievements are the consummation of holy aspirations. He who lives constantly in the conception of noble and lofty thoughts, who dwells upon all that is pure and unselfish, will, as surely as the sun reaches its zenith and the moon its full, become wise and noble in character, and rise into a position of influence and blessedness.

Achievement, of whatever kind, is the crown of effort, the diadem of thought. By the aid of self-control, resolution, purity, righteousness, and well-directed thought a man ascends; by the aid of animality, indolence, impurity, corruption, and confusion of thought a man descends.

A man may rise to high success in the world, and even to lofty altitudes in the spiritual realm, and again descend into weakness and wretchedness by allowing arrogant, selfish, and corrupt thoughts to take possession of him.

Victories attained by right thought can only be maintained by watchfulness. Many give way when success is assured, and rapidly fall back into failure.

All achievements, whether in the business, intellectual, or spiritual world, are the result of definitely directed thought, are governed by the same law and are of the same method; the only difference lies in *the object of attainment.*

He who would accomplish little must sacrifice little; he who would achieve much must sacrifice much; he who would attain highly must sacrifice greatly.

Visions
and Ideals

The dreamers are the saviors of the world. As the visible world is sustained by the invisible, so men, through all their trials and sins and sordid vocations, are nourished by the beautiful visions of their solitary dreamers. Humanity cannot forget its dreamers; it cannot let their ideals fade and die; it lives in them; it knows them as the *realities* which it shall one day see and know.

Composer, sculptor, painter, poet, prophet, sage, these are the makers of the afterworld, the architects of heaven. The world is beautiful because they have lived; without them, laboring humanity would perish.

He who cherishes a beautiful vision, a lofty ideal in his heart, will one day realize it. Columbus cherished a vision of another world, and he discovered it; Copernicus fostered the vision of a multiplicity of worlds and a wider universe, and he revealed it; Buddha beheld the vision of a spiritual world of stainless beauty and perfect peace, and he entered into it.

Cherish your visions; cherish your ideals; cherish the music that stirs in your heart, the beauty that forms in your mind, the loveliness that drapes your purest thoughts, for out of them will grow all delightful conditions, all heavenly environment; of these, if you but remain true to them, your world will at last be built.

To desire is to obtain; to aspire is to achieve. Shall man's basest desires receive the fullest measure of gratification, and his purest aspirations starve for lack of sustenance? Such is not the Law: such a condition of things can never obtain: "Ask and receive."

Dream lofty dreams, and as you dream, so shall you become. Your Vision is the promise of what you shall one day be; your Ideal is the prophecy of what you shall at last unveil.

The greatest achievement was at first and for a time a dream. The oak sleeps in the acorn; the bird waits in the egg; and in the highest vision of the soul a waking angel stirs. Dreams are the seed-lings of realities.

Your circumstances may be uncongenial, but they shall not long remain so if you but perceive an Ideal and strive to reach it. You cannot travel *within* and stand still *without*. Here is a youth hard pressed by poverty and labor; Confined long hours in an unhealthy workshop; unschooled, and lacking all the arts of refinement. But he dreams of better things: he thinks of intelligence, of refinement, of grace and beauty. He conceives of, mentally builds up, an ideal condition of life; the vision of a wider liberty and a larger scope takes possession of him; unrest urges him to action, and he utilizes all his spare time and means, small though they are, to the development of his latent powers and resources. Very soon so altered has his mind become that the workshop can no longer hold him. It has become so out of harmony with his mentality that it falls out of his life as a garment is cast aside, and, with the growth of opportunities which fit the scope of his expanding powers, he passes out of it forever. Years later we see this youth as a full-grown man. We find him a master of certain forces of the mind which he wields with world-wide influence and almost unequaled power. In his hands he holds the cords of gigantic responsibilities; he speaks, and lo! lives are changed; men and women hang upon his words and remold their characters, and, sunlike, he becomes the fixed and luminous center around which innumerable destinies revolve. He has realized the Vision of his youth. He has become one with his Ideal.

And you, too, youthful reader, will realize the Vision (not the idle wish) of your heart, be it base or beautiful, or a mixture of both, for you will always gravitate toward that which you, secretly, most love. Into your hands will be placed the exact results of your own thoughts; you will receive that which you earn; no more, no less. Whatever your present environment may be, you will fall, remain, or rise with your thoughts, your Vision, your Ideal. You will become as small as your controlling desire; as great as your dominant aspiration: in the beautiful words of Stanton Kirkham Davis, "You may be keeping accounts, and presently you shall walk out of the door that for so long has seemed to you the barrier of your ideals, and shall find yourself before an audience—the pen still behind your ear, the ink stains on your fingers—and then and there shall pour out the torrent of your inspiration. You may be driving sheep, and you shall wander to the city—bucolic and open mouthed; shall wander under the intrepid guidance of the spirit into the studio of the master, and after a time he shall say, 'I have nothing more to teach you.' And now you have become the master, who did so recently dream of great things while driving sheep. You shall lay down the saw and the plane to take upon yourself the regeneration of the world."

The thoughtless, the ignorant, and the indolent, seeing only the apparent effects of things and not the things themselves, talk of luck, of fortune, and chance. Seeing a man grow rich, they say, "How lucky he is!" Observing another become intellectual, they exclaim, "How highly favored he is!" And noting the saintly character and wide influence of another, they remark, "How chance aids him at every turn!" They do not see the trials and failures and struggles which these men have voluntarily encountered in order to gain their experience; have no knowledge of the sacrifices they have made, of the undaunted efforts they have put forth, of the faith they have exercised, that they might overcome the apparently insurmountable, and realize the Vision of their heart. They do not know the darkness and the heartaches; they only see the light and joy, and call it "luck"; do not see the long and arduous journey, but only behold the pleasant goal, and call it "good fortune"; do not understand the process, but only perceive the result, and call it "chance."

In all human affairs there are *efforts*, and there are *results*, and the strength of the effort is the measure of the result. Chance is not. "Gifts," powers, material, intellectual, and spiritual possessions are the fruits of effort; they are thoughts completed, objects accomplished, visions realized.

The Vision that you glorify in your mind, the Ideal that you enthrone in your heart—this you will build your life by, this you will become.

Serenity

Calmness of mind is one of the beautiful jewels of wisdom. It is the result of long and patient effort in self-control. Its presence is an indication of ripened experience, and of a more than ordinary knowledge of the laws and operations of thought.

A man becomes calm in the measure that he understands himself as a thought-evolved being, for such knowledge necessitates the understanding of others as the result of thought, and as he develops a right understanding, and sees more and more clearly the internal relations of things by the action of cause and effect, he ceases to fuss and fume and worry and grieve, and remains poised, steadfast, serene.

The calm man, having learned how to govern himself, knows how to adapt himself to others; and they, in turn, reverence his spiritual strength, and feel that they can learn of him and rely upon him. The more tranquil a man becomes, the greater is his success, his influence, his power for good. Even the ordinary trader will find his business prosperity increase as he develops a greater self-control and equanimity, for people will always prefer to deal with a man whose demeanor is strongly equable.

The strong, calm man is always loved and revered. He is like a shade-giving tree in a thirsty land, or a sheltering rock in a storm. "Who does not love a tranquil heart, a sweet-tempered, balanced life? It does not matter whether it rains or shines, or what changes come to those possessing these blessings, for they are always sweet, serene, and calm. That exquisite poise of character which we call serenity is the last lesson of culture; it is the flowering of life, the fruitage of the soul. It is precious as wisdom, more to be desired than gold— yea, than even fine gold. How insignificant mere money-seeking looks in comparison with a serene life—a life that dwells in the ocean of Truth, beneath the waves, beyond the reach of tempests, in the Eternal Calm!

"How many people we know who sour their lives, who ruin all that is sweet and beautiful by explosive tempers, who destroy their poise of character, and make bad blood! It is a question whether the great majority of people do not ruin their lives and mar their happiness by lack of self-control. How few people we meet in life who are well-balanced, who have that exquisite poise which is characteristic of the finished character!"

Yes, humanity surges with uncontrolled passion, is tumultuous with ungoverned grief, is blown about by anxiety and doubt. Only the wise man, only he whose thoughts are controlled and purified, makes the winds and the storms of the soul obey him.

Tempest-tossed souls, wherever ye may be, under whatsoever conditions ye may live, know this—in the ocean of life the isles of Blessedness are smiling, and the sunny shore of your ideal awaits your coming. Keep your hand firmly upon the helm of thought. In the bark of your soul reclines the commanding Master; He does but sleep; wake Him. Self-control is strength; Right Thought is mastery; Calmness is power. Say unto your heart, "Peace, be still!"

Above
Life's
Turmoil

Contents

Foreword

We cannot alter external things, nor shape other people to our liking, nor mould the world to our wishes but we can alter internal things—our desires, passions, thoughts—we can shape our liking to other people, and we can mould the inner world of our own mind in accordance with wisdom, and so reconcile it to the outer world of men and things. The turmoil of the world we cannot avoid, but the disturbances of mind we can overcome. The duties and difficulties of life claim our attention, but we can rise above all anxiety concerning them. Surrounded by noise, we can yet have a quiet mind; involved in responsibilities, the heart can be at rest; in the midst of strife, we can know the abiding peace. The twenty pieces which comprise this book, unrelated as some of them are in the letter, will be found to be harmonious in the spirit, in that they point the reader toward those heights of self-knowledge and self-conquest which, rising above the turbulence of the world, lift their peaks where the Heavenly Silence reigns.

—James Allen

True Happiness

To maintain an unchangeable sweetness of disposition, to think only thoughts that are pure and gentle, and to be happy under all circumstances—such blessed conditions and such beauty of character and life should be the aim of all, and particularly so of those who wish to lessen the misery of the world. If anyone has failed to lift *himself* above ungentleness, impurity, and unhappiness, he is greatly deluded if he imagines he can make the world happier by the propagation of any theory or theology. He who is daily living in harshness, impurity, or unhappiness is day by day adding to the sum of the world's misery; whereas he who continually lives in goodwill, and does not depart from happiness, is day by day increasing the sum of the world's happiness, and this independently of any religious beliefs which these may or may not hold.

He who has not learned how to be gentle, or giving, loving and happy, has learned very little, great though his book-learning and profound his acquaintance with the letter of Scripture may be, for it is in the process of *becoming* gentle, pure, and happy that the deep, real, and enduring lessons of life are learned. Unbroken sweetness of conduct in the face of all outward antagonism is the infallible indication of a self-conquered soul, the witness of wisdom, and the proof of the possession of Truth.

A sweet and happy soul is the ripened fruit of experience and wisdom, and it sheds abroad the invisible yet powerful aroma of its influence, gladdening the hearts of others, and purifying the world. And all who will, and who have not yet commenced, may begin *this day* if they will so resolve, to live sweetly and happily, as becomes the dignity of a true manhood or womanhood. Do not say that your surroundings are against you. A man's surroundings are *never* against him; they are there to aid him, and all those outward occurrences over which you lose sweetness and peace of mind are the very conditions necessary to your development, and it is only by meeting and overcoming them that you can learn, and grow, and ripen. The fault is in yourself.

Pure happiness is the rightful and healthy condition of the soul, and all may possess it if they will live purely and unselfishly.

Have goodwill
To all that lives, letting unkindness die,
And greed and wrath, so that your lives be made
Like soft airs passing by.

Is this too difficult for you? Then unrest and unhappiness will continue to dwell with you. Your belief and aspiration and resolve are all that are necessary to make it easy, to render it in the near future a thing accomplished, a blessed state realised.

Despondency, irritability, anxiety and complaining, condemning and grumbling—all these are thought-cankers, mind-diseases; they are the indications of a wrong mental condition, and those who suffer therefrom would do well to remedy their thinking and conduct. It is true there is much sin and misery in the world, so that all our love and compassion are needed, *but our misery is not needed*—there is already too much of that. No, it is our cheerfulness and happiness that are needed for there is too little of that. We can give nothing better to the world than beauty of life and character; without this, all other things are vain; this is pre-eminently excellent; it is enduring, real, and not to be overthrown, and it includes all joy and blessedness.

Cease to dwell pessimistically upon the wrongs around you; dwell no more in complaints about, and revolt against, the evil in others, and commence to live free from all wrong and evil yourself. Peace of mind, pure religion, and true reform lie this way. If you would have others true, be true; if you would have the world emancipated from misery and sin, emancipate yourself; if you would have your home and your surroundings happy, be happy. You can transform everything around you if you will transform yourself.

Don't bewail and bemoan. . . .
Don't waste yourself in rejection, nor bark
*   against the bad, but chant the beauties*
*   of the good.*

And this you will naturally and spontaneously do as you realise the good in yourself.

The Immortal Man

Immortality is here and now, and is not a speculative something beyond the grave. It is a lucid state of consciousness in which the sensations of the body, the varying and unrestful states of mind, and the circumstances and events of life are seen to be of a fleeting and therefore of an illusory character.

Immortality does not belong to time, and will never be found in time; it belongs to Eternity; and just as time is here and now, so is Eternity here and now, and a man may find that Eternity and establish in it, if he will overcome the self that derives its life from the unsatisfying and perishable things of time.

Whilst a man remains immersed in sensation, desire, and the passing events of his day-by-day existence, and regards those sensations, desires, and passing events as of the essence of himself, he can have no knowledge of immortality. The thing which such a man desires, and which he mistakes for immortality, is *persistence*; that is, a continuous succession of sensations and events in time. Living in, loving, and clinging to the things which stimulate and minister to his immediate gratification, and realising no state of consciousness above and independent of this, he thirsts for its continuance, and strives to banish the thought that he will at last have to part from those earthly luxuries and delights to which he has become enslaved, and which he regards as being inseparable from himself.

Persistence is the antithesis of immortality; and to be absorbed in it is spiritual death. Its very nature is change, impermanence. It is a continual living and dying.

The death of the body can never bestow upon a man immortality. Spirits are not different from men, and live their little feverish life of broken consciousness, and are still immersed in change and mortality. The mortal man, he who thirsts for the persistence of his pleasure-loving personality, is still mortal after death, and only lives another life with a beginning and an end without memory of the past, or knowledge of the future.

The immortal man is he who has detached himself from the things of time by having ascended into that state of consciousness which is fixed and unvariable, and is not affected by passing events and sensations. Human life consists of an evermoving procession of events, and in this procession the mortal man is immersed, and he is carried along with it; and being so carried along, he has no knowledge of what is behind and before him. The immortal man is he who has stepped out of this procession, and he stands by unmoved and watches it; and from his fixed place he sees both the before, the behind, and the middle of the moving thing called life. No longer identifying himself with the sensations and fluctuations of the personality, or with the outward changes which make up the life in time, he has become the passionless spectator of his own destiny and of the destinies of men and nations.

The mortal man, also, is one who is caught in a dream, and he neither knows that he was formerly awake, nor that he will wake again; he is a dreamer without knowledge, nothing more. The immortal man is as one who has awakened out of his dream, and he knows that his dream was not an enduring reality, but a passing illusion. He is a man with knowledge, the knowledge of both states—that of persistence, and that of immortality—and is in full possession of himself.

The mortal man lives in the time or world state of consciousness which begins and ends; the immortal man lives in the cosmic or heaven state of consciousness, in which there is neither beginning nor end, but an eternal now. Such a man remains poised and steadfast under all changes, and the death of his body will not in any way interrupt the eternal consciousness in which he abides. Of such a one it is said, "He shall not taste of death," because he has stepped out of the stream of mortality, and established himself in the abode of Truth. Bodies, personalities, nations, and worlds pass away, but Truth remains, and its glory is undimmed by time. The immortal man, then, is he who has conquered himself, who no longer identifies himself with the self-seeking forces of the personality, but who has trained himself to direct those forces with the hand of a master, and so has brought them into harmony with the causal energy and source of all things.

The fret and fever of life has ceased, doubt and fear are cast out, and death is not for him who has realised the fadeless splendour of that life of Truth by adjusting heart and mind to the eternal and unchangeable verities.

The Overcoming
of Self

Many people have very confused and erroneous ideas concerning the terms *"the overcoming of self," "the eradication of desire,"* and *"the annihilation of the personality."* Some (particularly the intellectual who are prone to theories) regard it as a metaphysical theory altogether apart from life and conduct; while others conclude that it is the crushing out of all life, energy and action, and the attempt to idealise stagnation and death. These errors and confusions, arising as they do in the minds of individuals, can only be removed by the individuals themselves; but perhaps it may make their removal a little less difficult (for those who are seeking Truth) by presenting the matter in another way.

The doctrine of the overcoming or annihilation of self is simplicity itself, indeed, so simple, practical, and close at hand is it that a child of five, whose mind has not yet become clouded with theories, theological schemes and speculative philosophies, would be far more likely to comprehend it than many older people who have lost their hold upon simple and beautiful truths by the adoption of complicated theories.

The annihilation of self consists in weeding out and destroying all those elements in the soul which lead to division, strife, suffering, disease and sorrow. It does not mean the destruction of any good and beautiful and peace-producing quality. For instance, when a man is tempted to irritability or anger, and by a great effort overcomes the selfish tendency, casts it from him, and acts from the spirit of patience and love, in that moment of self-conquest he practises the annihilation of self. Every noble man practises it in part, though he may deny it in his words, and he who carries out this practice to its completion, eradicating every selfish tendency until only the divinely beautiful qualities remain, he is said to annihilated the personality (all the personal elements) and to have arrived at Truth.

The self which is to be annihilated is composed of the following ten worthless and sorrow-producing elements:

Lust	*Vanity*
Hatred	*Pride*
Avarice	*Doubt*
Self-indulgence	*Dark belief*
Self-seeking	*Delusion*

It is the total abandonment, the complete annihilation of these ten elements, for they comprise the body of desire. On the other hand it teaches the cultivation, practise, and preservation of the following ten divine qualities:

Purity	*Fearlessness*
Patience	*Knowledge*
Humility	*Wisdom*
Self-sacrifice	*Compassion*
Self-reliance	*Love*

These comprise the Body of Truth, and to live entirely in them is to be a doer and knower of the Truth, is to be an embodiment of Truth. The combination of the ten elements is called *Self* or *the Personality*; the combination of the ten qualities produces what is called Truth; the Impersonal; the abiding, real and immortal Man.

It will thus be seen that it is not the destruction of any noble, true, and enduring quality that is taught, but only the destruction of those things that are ignoble, false and evanescent. Neither is this overcoming of self the deprivation of gladness, happiness and joy, but rather is it the constant possession of these things by living in the joy-begetting qualities. It is the abandonment of the *lust* for enjoyment, but not of enjoyment itself; the destruction of the thirst for pleasure, but not of pleasure itself; the annihilation of the *selfish longing* for love, and power, and possessions themselves. It is the preservation of all those things which draw and bind men together in unity and concord, and, far from idealising stagnation and death, urges men to the practise of those qualities which lead to the highest, noblest, most effective, and enduring action. He whose actions proceed from some or all of the ten elements wastes his energies upon negations, and does not preserve his soul; but he whose actions proceed from some or all of the ten qualities, he truly and wisely acts and so preserves his soul.

He who lives largely in the ten earthly elements, and who is blind and deaf to the spiritual verities, will find no attraction in the doctrine of self-surrender, for it will appear to him as the complete extinction of his being; but he who is endeavouring to live in the ten heavenly qualities will see the glory and beauty of the doctrine, and will know it as the foundation of Life Eternal. He will also see that when men apprehend and practise it, industry, commerce, government, and every worldly activity will be purified; and action, purpose and intelligence, instead of being destroyed, will be intensified and enlarged, but freed from strife and pain.

The Uses of Temptation

The soul, in its journey toward perfection, passes through three distinct stages. The first is the *animal* stage, in which the man is content to live, in the gratification of his senses, unawakened to the knowledge of sin, or of his divine inheritance, and altogether unconscious of the spiritual possibilities within himself.

The second is the *dual* stage, in which the mind is continually oscillating between its animal and divine tendencies having become awakened to the consciousness of both. It is during this stage that temptation plays its part in the progress of the soul. It is a stage of continual fighting, of falling and rising, of sinning and repenting, for the man, still loving, and reluctant to leave, the gratifications in which he has so long lived, yet also aspires to the purity and excellence of the spiritual state, and he is continually mortified by an undecided choice.

Urged on by the divine life within him, this stage becomes at last one of deep anguish and suffering, and then the soul is ushered into the third stage, that of *knowledge*, in which the man rises above both sin and temptation, and enters into peace.

Temptation, like contentment in sin, is not a lasting condition, as the majority of people suppose; it is a passing phase, an experience through which the soul must pass; but as to whether a man will pass through that condition in this present life, and realise holiness and heavenly rest here and now, will depend entirely upon the strength of his intellectual and spiritual exertions, and upon the intensity and ardour with which he searches for Truth.

Temptation, with all its attendant torments can be overcome here and now, but it can only be overcome by knowledge. It is a condition of darkness or of semi-darkness. The fully enlightened soul is proof against all temptation. When a man fully understands the source, nature, and meaning of temptation, in that hour he will conquer it, and will rest from his long travail; but whilst he remains in ignorance, attention to religious observances, and much praying and reading of Scripture will fail to bring him peace.

If a man goes out to conquer an enemy, knowing nothing of his enemy's strength, tactics, or place of ambush, he will not only ignominiously fail, but will speedily fall into the hands of the enemy. He who would overcome his enemy the tempter, must discover his stronghold and place of concealment, and must also find out the unguarded gates in his own fortress where his enemy effects so easy an entrance. This necessitates continual meditation, ceaseless watchfulness, and constant and rigid introspection which lays bare, before the spiritual eyes of the tempted one, the vain and selfish motives of his soul. This is the holy warfare of the saints; it is the fight upon which every soul enters when it awakens out of its long sleep of animal indulgence.

Men fail to conquer, and the fight is indefinitely prolonged, because they labour, almost universally, under two delusions: first, that all temptations come from without; and second, that they are tempted because of their goodness. Whilst a man is held in bondage by these two delusions, he will make no progress; when he has shaken them off, he will pass on rapidly from victory to victory, and will taste of spiritual joy and rest.

Two searching truths must take the place of these two delusions, and those truths are: first, that *all temptation comes from within*; and second, that *a man is tempted because of the evil that is within him*. The idea that God, a devil, evil spirits, or outward objects are the source of temptation must be dispelled.

The source and cause of all temptation is in the *inward desire*; that being purified or eliminated, outward objects and extraneous powers are utterly powerless to move the soul to sin or to temptation. The outward object is merely the *occasion* of the temptation, *never the cause*; this is in the desire of the one tempted. If the cause existed in the object, all men would be tempted alike, temptation could never be overcome, and men would be hopelessly doomed to endless torment; but seated, as it is, in his own desires, he has the remedy in his own hands, and can become victorious over all temptation by purifying those desires. A man is tempted because there are within him certain desires or states of mind which he has come to regard as unholy. These desires may lie asleep for a long time, and the man may think that he has got rid of them, when suddenly, on the presentation of an outward object, the sleeping desire wakes up and thirsts of immediate gratification; and this is the state of temptation.

The good in a man is never tempted. Goodness destroys temptation. It is the evil in a man that is aroused and tempted. The measure of a man's temptations is the exact register of his own unholiness.

As a man purifies his heart, temptation ceases, for when a certain unlawful desire has been taken out of the heart, the object which formerly appealed to it can no longer do so, but becomes dead and powerless, for there is nothing left in the heart that can respond to it. The honest man cannot be tempted to steal, let the occasion be ever so opportune; the man of purified appetites cannot be tempted to gluttony and drunkenness, though the viands and wines be the most luscious; he of an enlightened understanding, whose mind is calm in the strength of inward virtue, can never be tempted to anger, irritability or revenge, and the wiles and charms of the wanton fall upon the purified heart as empty meaningless shadows.

Temptation shows a man just where he is sinful and ignorant, and is a means of urging him on to higher altitudes of knowledge and purity. Without temptation the soul cannot grow and become strong, there could be no wisdom, no real virtue; and though there would be lethargy and death, there could be no peace and no fulness of life. When temptation is understood and conquered, perfection is assured, and such perfection may become any man's who is willing to cast every selfish and impure desire by which he is possessed, into the sacrificial fire of knowledge. Let men, therefore, search diligently for Truth, realising that whilst they are subject to temptation, they have not comprehended Truth, and have much to learn.

Ye who are tempted know, then, that ye are tempted of yourselves. "For every man is tempted when he is drawn away of his own lusts," says the Apostle James. You are tempted because you are clinging to the animal within you and are unwilling to let go; because you are living in the false mortal self which is ever devoid of all true knowledge, knowing nothing, seeking nothing, but its own immediate gratification, ignorant of every Truth, and of every divine Principle. Clinging to that self, you continually suffer the pains of three separate torments; the torment of desire, the torment of repletion, and the torment of remorse.

So flameth Trishna, lust and thirst of things.
Eager, ye cleave to shadows, dote on dreams;
A false self in the midst ye plant, and make
A World around which seems;
Blind to the height beyond; deaf to the sound
Of sweet airs breathed from far past Indra's sky;
Dumb to the summons of the true life kept

For him who false puts by,
So grow the strifes and lusts which make earth's
     war,
So grieve poor cheated hearts and flow salt tears;
So wax the passions, envies, angers, hates;
So years chase blood-stained years
With wild red feet.

In that false self lies the germ of every suffering, the blight of every hope, the substance of every grief. When you are ready to give it up; when you are willing to have laid bare before you all its selfishness, impurity, and ignorance, and to confess its darkness to the uttermost, then will you enter upon the life of self-knowledge and self-mastery, you will become conscious of the god within you, of that divine nature which, seeking no gratification, abides in a region of perpetual joy and peace where suffering cannot come and where temptation can find no foothold. Establishing yourself, day by day, more and more firmly in that inward Divinity, the time will at last come when you will be able to say with Him whom millions worship, few understand and fewer still follow—"The Prince of this world cometh and hath nothing in me."

The Man
of Integrity

There are times in the life of every man who takes his stand on high moral principles when his faith in, and knowledge of, those principles is tested to the uttermost, and the way in which he comes out of the fiery trial decides as to whether he has sufficient strength to live as a man of Truth, and join the company of the free, or shall still remain a slave and a hireling to the cruel taskmaster, Self.

Such times of trial generally assume the form of a temptation to do a wrong thing and continue in comfort and prosperity, or to stand by what is right and accept poverty and failure; and so powerful is the trial that, to the tempted one, it plainly appears on the face of things as though, if he chooses the wrong, his material success will be assured for the remainder of his life, but if he does what is right, he will be ruined for ever.

Frequently the man at once quails and gives way before this appalling prospect which the Path of Righteousness seems to hold out for him, but should he prove sufficiently strong to withstand this onslaught of temptation, then the inward seducer the spirit of self, assumes the grab of an Angel of Light, and whispers, "Think of your wife and children; think of those who are dependent upon you; will you bring them down to disgrace and starvation?"

Strong indeed and pure must be the man who can come triumphant out of such a trial, but he who does so, enters at once a higher realm of life, where his spiritual eyes are opened to see beautiful things; and then poverty and ruin which seemed inevitable do not come, but a more abiding success comes, and a peaceful heart and a quiet conscience. But he who fails does not obtain the promised prosperity, and his heart is restless and his conscience troubled.

The right-doer cannot ultimately fail, the wrong-doer cannot ultimately succeed, for

Such is the Law which moves to Righteousness
Which none at last can turn aside or stay,

and it is because justice is at the heart of things—because the Great Law is good—that the man of integrity is superior to fear, and failure, and poverty, and shame, and disgrace. As the poet further says of this Law:

The heart of its Love, the end of it
Is peace and consummation sweet-obey.

The man who fearing the loss of present pleasures or material comforts, denies the Truth within him, can be injured, and robbed, and degraded, and trampled upon, because he has first injured, robbed and degraded, and trampled upon his own nobler self; but the man of steadfast virtue, of unblemished integrity, cannot be subject to such conditions, because he has denied the craven self within him and has taken refuge in Truth. It is not the scourge and the chains which make a man a slave, but the fact that he *is* a slave.

Slander, accusation, and malice cannot affect the righteous man, nor call from him any bitter response, nor does he need to go about to defend himself and prove his innocence. His innocence and integrity alone are a sufficient answer to all that hatred may attempt against him. Nor can he ever be subdued by the forces of darkness, having subdued all those forces within himself, but he turns all evil things to good account—out of darkness he brings light, out of hatred love, out of dishonour honour; and slanders, envies, and misrepresentations only serve to make more bright the jewel of Truth within him, and to glorify his high and holy destiny.

Let the man of integrity rejoice and be glad when he is severely tried; let him be thankful that he has been given an opportunity of proving his loyalty to the noble principles which he has espoused; and let him think: "Now is the hour of holy opportunity! Now is the day of triumph for Truth! Though I lose the whole world I will not desert the right!" So thinking, he will return good for evil, and will think compassionately of the wrongdoer.

The slanderer, the backbiter, and the wrongdoer may seem to succeed for a time, but the Law of Justice prevails; the man of integrity may seem to fail for a time, but he is invincible, and in none of the worlds, visible or invisible, can there be forged a weapon that shall prevail against him.

Discrimination

There is one quality which is pre-eminently necessary to spiritual development, the quality of discrimination.

A man's spiritual progress will be painfully slow and uncertain until there opens with him the eye of discrimination, for without this testing, proving, searching quality, he will but grope in the dark, will be unable to distinguish the real from the unreal, the shadow from the substance, and will so confuse the false with the true as to mistake the inward promptings of his animal nature for those of the spirit of Truth.

A blind man left in a strange place may go grope his way in darkness, but not without much confusion and many painful falls and bruisings.

Without discrimination a man is mentally blind, and his life is a painful groping in darkness, a confusion in which vice and virtue are indistinguishable one from the other, where facts are confounded with truths; opinions with principles, and where ideas, events, men, and things appear to be out of all relation to each other.

A man's mind and life should be free from confusion. He should be prepared to meet every mental, material and spiritual difficulty, and should not be inextricably caught (as many are) in the meshes of doubt, indecision and uncertainty when troubles and so-called misfortunes come along. He should be fortified against every emergency that can come against him; but such mental preparedness and strength cannot be attained in any degree without discrimination, and discrimination can only be developed by bringing into play and constantly exercising the analytical faculty.

Mind, like muscle, is developed by use, and the assiduous exercise of the mind in any given direction will develop, in that direction, mental capacity and power. The merely *critical* faculty is developed and strengthened by continuously comparing and analysing the ideas and opinions of others.

But discrimination is something more and greater than criticism; it is a spiritual quality from which the cruelty and egotism which so frequently accompany criticism are eliminated, and by virtue of which a man sees things as they are, and not as he would like them to be.

Discrimination, being a spiritual quality, can only be developed by spiritual methods, namely, by questioning, examining, and analysing one's own ideas, opinions, and conduct. The critical, fault finding faculty must be withdrawn from its merciless application to the opinions and conduct of others, and must be applied, with undiminished severity, to oneself. A man must be prepared to question his every opinion, his every thought, and his every line of conduct, and rigorously and logically test them; only in this way can the discrimination which destroys confusion will be developed.

Before a man can enter upon such mental exercise, he must make himself of a *teachable* spirit. This does not mean that he must allow himself to be led by others; it means that he must be prepared to yield up any cherished thoughts to which he clings, if it will not bear the penetrating light of reason, if it shrivels up before the pure flames of searching aspirations. The man who says, "I am right!" and who refuses to question his position in order to discover whether he is right, will continue to follow the line of his passions and prejudices, and will not acquire discrimination. The man who humbly asks, "Am I right?" and then proceeds to test and prove his position by earnest thought and the love of Truth, will always be able to discover the true and to distinguish it from the false, and he will acquire the priceless possession of discrimination.

The man who is afraid to think searchingly upon his opinions, and to reason critically upon his position, will have to develop moral courage before he can acquire discrimination.

A man must be true to himself, fearless with himself, before he can perceive the Pure Principles of Truth, before he can receive the all-revealing Light of Truth.

The more Truth is inquired of, the brighter it shines; it cannot suffer under examination and analysis.

The more error is questioned, the darker it grows; it cannot survive the entrance of pure and searching thought.

To "prove all things" is to find the good and throw the evil.

He who reasons and meditates learns to discriminate; he who discriminates discovers the eternally True.

Confusion, suffering and spiritual darkness follow the thoughtless.

Harmony, blessedness and the Light of Truth attend upon the thoughtful.

Passion and prejudice are blind, and cannot discriminate: they are still crucifying *the Christ* and releasing *Barabbas*.

Belief: The Basis of Action

Belief is an important word in the teachings of the wise, and it figures prominently in all religions. According to Jesus, a certain kind of belief is necessary to salvation or regeneration, and Buddha definitely taught that *right belief* is the first and most essential step in the Way of Truth, as without right belief there cannot be right conduct, and he who has not learned how to rightly govern and conduct himself, has not yet comprehended the simplest rudiments of Truth.

Belief as laid down by the Great Teachers, is not belief in any particular school, philosophy, or religion, but consists of *an altitude of mind determining the whole course of one's life*. Belief and conduct are, therefore inseparable, for the one determines the other.

Belief is the basis of all action, and, this being so, the belief which dominates the hearts or mind is shown in the life. Every man acts, thinks, lives in exact accordance with the belief which is rooted in his innermost being, and such is the mathematical nature of the laws which govern mind that it is absolutely impossible for anyone to believe in two opposing conditions at the same time. For instance, it is impossible to believe in justice and injustice, hatred and love, peace and strife, self and truth. Every man believes in one or the other of these opposites, *never in both*, and the daily conduct of every man indicates the nature of his belief. The man who believes in justice, who regards it as an eternal and indestructible Principle, never boils over with righteous indignation, does not grow cynical and pessimistic over the inequalities of life, and remains calm and untroubled through all trials and difficulties. It is impossible for him to act otherwise, for he believes that justice reigns, and that, therefore, all that is called injustice is fleeting and illusory.

The man who is continually getting enraged over the injustice of his fellow men, who talks about himself being badly treated, or who mourns over the lack of justice in the world around him, shows by his conduct, his attitude of mind, that he believes in injustice. However he may protest to the contrary, in his inmost heart he believes that confusion and chaos are dominant in the universe, the result being that he dwells in misery and unrest, and his conduct is faulty.

Again, he who believes in love, in its stability and power, *practises it under all circumstances*, never deviates from it, and bestows it alike upon enemies as upon friends. He who slanders and condemns, who speaks disparagingly of others, or regards them with contempt, believes not in love, but hatred; all his actions prove it, even though with tongue or pen he may eulogise love.

The believer in peace is known by his peaceful conduct. It is impossible for him to engage in strife. If attacked he does not retaliate, for he has seen the majesty of the angel of peace, and he can no longer pay homage to the demon of strife. The stirrer-up of strife, the lover of argument, he who rushes into self-defence upon any or every provocation, believes in strife, and will have naught to do with peace.

Further, he who believes in Truth renounces himself—that is, he refuses to centre his life in those passions, desires, and characteristics which crave only their own gratification, and by thus renouncing he becomes steadfastly fixed in Truth, and lives a wise, beautiful, and blameless life. The believer in self is known by his daily indulgences, gratifications, and vanities, and by the disappointments, sorrows, and mortifications which he continually suffers.

The believer in Truth does not suffer, for he has given up that self which is the cause of such suffering.

It will be seen by the foregoing that every man believes either in permanent and eternal Principles directing human life toward law and harmony, or in the negation of those Principles, with the resultant chaos in human affairs and in his own life.

Belief in the divine Principles of Justice, Compassion, Love, constitutes the *right belief* laid down by Buddha as being the basis of *right conduct*, and also the *belief unto salvation* as emphasised in the Christian Scriptures, for he who so believes cannot do otherwise than build his whole life upon these Principles, and so purifies his heart, and perfects his life.

Belief in the negation of this divine principle constitutes what is called in all religious *unbelief* and this unbelief is manifested as a sinful, troubled, and imperfect life.

Where there is Right Belief there is a blameless and perfect life; where there is false belief there is sin, there is sorrow, the mind and life are improperly governed, and there is affliction and unrest. "By their fruits ye shall know them."

There is much talk about, "belief in Jesus," but what does belief in Jesus mean? It means belief in his words, in the Principles he enunciated—and lived, in his commandments and in his exemplary life of perfection. He who declares belief in Jesus, and yet is all the time living in his lusts and indulgences, or in the spirit of hatred and condemnation, is self deceived. He believes not in Jesus. He believes in his own animal self. As a faithful servant delights in carrying out the commands of his master, so he who believes in Jesus carries out his commandments, and so is saved from sin. The supreme test of belief in Jesus is this: *Do I keep his commandments?* And this test is applied by St. John himself in the following words: "He that saith. I know him (Jesus), and *keepeth not His Commandments*, is a liar, and the truth is not in him. But whoso keepeth his word, in him verily is the word of God perfected."

It will be found after a rigid and impartial analysis, that *belief* lies at the root of all human conduct. Every thought, every act, every habit, is the direct outcome of a certain fixed belief, and one's conduct alters only as one's beliefs are modified. What we cling to, in that we believe; what we practise, in that we believe. When our belief in a thing ceases, we can no longer cling to or practise it; it falls away from us as a garment out-worn. Men cling to their lusts, and lies, and vanities, because they believe in them, believe there is gain and happiness in them. When they transfer their belief to the divine qualities of purity and humility, those sins trouble them no more.

Men are saved from error by belief in the supremacy of Truth. They are saved from sin by belief in Holiness or Perfection. They are saved from evil by belief in Good, for every belief is manifested in the life. It is not necessary to inquire as to a man's theological belief, for that is of little or no account, for what can it avail a man to believe that Jesus died for him, or that Jesus is God, or that he is "justified by faith," if he continues to live in his lower, sinful nature? All that is necessary to ask is this: "How does a man live?" "How does he conduct himself under trying circumstances?" The answer to these questions will show whether a man believes in the power of evil or in the power of Good.

He who believes in the power of Good, lives a good, spiritual, or godly life, for Goodness is God, yea, verily is God Himself, and he will soon leave behind him all sins and sorrows who believes, with steadfast and unwavering faith, in the Supreme Good.

The Belief That Saves

It has been said that a man's whole life and character is the outcome of his *belief*, and also that his *belief* has nothing whatever to do with his life. *Both statements are true.* The confusion and contradiction of these two statements are only apparent, and are quickly dispelled when it is remembered that there are *two entirely distinct kinds of belief*, namely, *Head-belief* and *Heart-belief*.

Head, or intellectual belief, is not fundamental and causative, but it is superficial and consequent, and that it has no power in the moulding of a man's character, the most superficial observer may easily see. Take, for instance, half a dozen men from any creed. They not only hold the same theological belief, but confess the same articles of faith in every particular, and yet their characters are vastly different. One will be just as noble as another is ignoble; one will be mild and gentle, another coarse and irascible; one will be honest, another dishonest; one will indulge certain habits which another will rigidly abjure, and so on, plainly indicating that theological belief is not an influential factor in a man's life.

A man's theological belief is merely his intellectual opinion or view of the universe; God, The Bible, etc, and behind and underneath this head-belief there lies, deeply rooted in his innermost being, the hidden, silent, *secret belief of his heart*, and it is this belief which moulds and makes his whole life. It is this which makes those six men who, whilst holding the same theology, are yet so vastly at variance in their deeds—*they differ in the vital belief of the heart.*

What, then, is this heart-belief?

It is that which a man loves and clings to and fosters in his soul; for he thus loves and clings to and fosters in his heart, because he *believes* in them, and believing in them and loving them, he practises them; thus is his life the effect of his *belief,* but it has no relation to the particular creed which comprises his intellectual belief. One man clings to impure and immoral things because he believes in them; another does not cling to them because he has ceased to believe in them. A man cannot cling to anything unless he believes in it; belief always precedes action, therefore a man's deeds and life are the fruits of his belief.

The Priest and the Levite who passed by the injured and helpless man, held, no doubt, very strongly to the theological doctrines of their fathers—that was their intellectual belief—but in their hearts they did not believe in mercy, and so lived and acted accordingly. The good Samaritan may or may not have had any theological beliefs nor was it necessary that he should have; but in his heart he believed in mercy, and acted accordingly.

Strictly speaking, there are only two beliefs which vitally affect the life, and they are, *belief in good* and *belief in evil.*

He who believes in all those things that are good, will love them, and live in them; he who believes in those things that are impure and selfish, will love them, and cling to them. The tree is known by its fruits.

A man's beliefs about God, Jesus, and the Bible are one thing; his life, as bound up in his actions, is another; therefore a man's theological belief is of no consequence; but the thoughts which he harbours, his attitude of mind toward others, and his actions, these, and these only, determine and demonstrate whether the belief of a man's heart is fixed in the false or true.

Thought
and Action

As the fruit to the tree and the water to the spring, so is action to thought. It does not come into manifestation suddenly and without a cause. It is the result of a long and silent growth; the end of a hidden process which has long been gathering force. The fruit of the tree and the water gushing from the rock are both the effect of a combination of natural processes in air and earth which have long worked together in secret to produce the phenomenon; and the beautiful acts of enlightenment and the dark deeds of sin are both the ripened effects of trains of thought which have long been harboured in the mind.

The sudden falling, when greatly tempted, into some grievous sin by one who was believed, and who probably believed himself, to stand firm, is seen neither to be a *sudden* nor a causeless thing when the hidden process of thought which led up to it are revealed. The *falling* was merely the end, the outworking, the finished result of what commenced in the mind probably years before.

The man had allowed a wrong thought to enter his mind; and a second and a third time he had welcomed it, and allowed it to nestle in his heart. Gradually he became accustomed to it, and cherished, and fondled, and tended it; and so it grew, until at last it attained such strength and force that it attracted to itself the opportunity which enabled it to burst forth and ripen into act. As falls the stately building whose foundations have been gradually undermined by the action of water, so at last falls the strong man who allows corrupt thoughts to creep into his mind and secretly undermine his character.

When it is seen that all sin and temptation are the natural outcome of the thoughts of the individual, the way to overcome sin and temptation becomes plain, and its achievement a near possibility, and, sooner or later, a certain reality, for if a man will admit, cherish, and brood upon thoughts that are pure and good, those thoughts, just as surely as the impure, will grow and gather force, and will at last attract to themselves the opportunities which will enable them to ripen into act.

"There is nothing hidden that shall not be revealed," and every thought that is harboured in the mind must, by virtue of the impelling force which is inherent in the universe, at last blossom into act good or bad according to its nature. The divine Teacher and the sensualist are both the product of their own thoughts, and have become what they are as the result of the seeds of thought which they have implanted, are allowed to fall, into the garden of the heart, and have afterwards watered, tended, and cultivated.

Let no man think he can overcome sin and temptation by wrestling with opportunity; he can only overcome them by purifying his thoughts; and if he will, day by day, in the silence of his soul, and in the performance of his duties, strenuously overcome all erroneous inclination, and put in its place thoughts that are true and that will endure the light, opportunity to do evil will give place to opportunity for accomplishing good, for a man can only attract that to him which is in harmony with his nature, and no temptation can gravitate to a man unless there is that in his heart which is capable of responding to it.

Guard well your thoughts, reader, for what you really are in your secret thoughts today, be it good or evil, you will, sooner or later, *become* in actual deed. He who unwearyingly guards the portals of his mind against the intrusion of sinful thoughts, and occupies himself with loving thoughts, with pure, strong, and beautiful thoughts, will, when the season of their ripening comes, bring forth the fruits of gentle and holy deeds, and no temptation that can come against him shall find him unarmed or unprepared.

Your Mental
Attitude

As a being of thought, your dominant mental attitude will determine your condition in life. It will also be the gauge of your knowledge and the measures of your attainment. The so-called limitations of your nature are the boundary lines of your thoughts; they are self-erected fences, and can be drawn to a narrower circle, extended to a wider, or be allowed to remain.

You are the thinker of your thoughts and as such you are the maker of yourself and condition. Thought is causal and creative, and appears in your character and life in the form of results. There are no accidents in your life. Both its harmonies and antagonisms are the responsive echoes of your thoughts. A man thinks, and his life appears.

If your dominant mental attitude is peaceable and lovable, bliss and blessedness will follow you; if it be resistant and hateful, trouble and distress will cloud your pathway. Out of ill-will will come grief and disaster; out of good-will, healing and reparation.

You imagine your circumstances as being separate from yourself, but they are intimately related to your thought world. Nothing appears without an adequate cause. Everything that happens is just. Nothing is fated, everything is formed.

As you think, you travel; as you love, you attract. You are today where your thoughts have brought you; you will be to-morrow where your thoughts take you. You cannot escape the result of your thoughts, but you can endure and learn, can accept and be glad.

You will always come to the place where your *love* (your most abiding and intense thought) can receive its measure of gratification. If your love be base, you will come to a base place; if it be beautiful, you will come to a beautiful place.

You can alter your thoughts, and so alter your condition. Strive to perceive the vastness and grandeur of your responsibility. You are powerful, not powerless. You are as powerful to obey as you are to disobey; as strong to be pure as to be impure; as ready for wisdom as for ignorance. You can learn what you will, can remain as ignorant as you choose. If you love knowledge you will obtain it; if you love wisdom you will secure it; if you love purity you will realise it. All things await your acceptance, and you choose by the thoughts which you entertain. A man remains ignorant because he loves ignorance, and chooses ignorant thoughts; a man becomes wise because he loves wisdom and chooses wise thoughts. No man is hindered by another; he is only hindered by himself. No man suffers because of another, he suffers only because of himself. By the noble Gateway of Pure Thought you can enter the highest Heaven; by the ignoble doorway of impure thought you can descend into the lowest hell.

Your mental attitude toward others will faithfully react upon yourself, and will manifest itself in every relation of your life. Every impure and selfish thought that you send out comes back to you in your circumstances in some form of suffering; every pure and unselfish thought returns to you in some form of blessedness. Your circumstances are *effects* of which the cause is inward and invisible. As the father-mother of your thoughts you are the maker of your state and condition. When you know yourself, you will perceive, that every event in your life is weighed in the faultless balance of equity. When you understand the law within your mind you will cease to regard yourself as the impotent and blind tool of circumstances, and will become the strong and seeing master.

Sowing and Reaping

Go into the fields and country lanes in the spring-time, and you will see farmers and gardeners busy sowing seeds in the newly prepared soil. If you were to ask any one of those gardeners or farmers what kind of produce he expected from the seed he was sowing, he would doubtless regard you as foolish, and would tell you that he does not "expect" at all, that it is a matter of common knowledge that his produce will be of the kind which he is sowing, and that he is sowing wheat, or barley, or turnips, as the case may be, in order to reproduce that particular kind.

Every fact and process in Nature contains a moral lesson for the wise man. There is no law in the world of Nature around us which is not to be found operating with the same mathematical certainty in the mind of man and in human life. All the parables of Jesus are illustrative of this truth, and are drawn from the simple facts of Nature. There is a process of seed-sowing in the mind and life a spiritual sowing which leads to a harvest according to the kind of seed sown. Thoughts, words, and acts are seeds sown, and, by the inviolable law of things, they produce after their kind.

The man who thinks hateful thoughts brings hatred upon himself. The man who thinks loving thoughts is loved. The man whose thoughts, words and acts are sincere, is surrounded by sincere friends; the insincere man is surrounded by insincere friends. The man who sows wrong thoughts and deeds, and prays that God will bless him, is in the position of a farmer who, having sown tares, asks God to bring forth for him a harvest of wheat.

> *That which ye sow, ye reap; see yonder fields*
> *The sesamum was sesamum, the corn*
> *Was corn; the silence and the darkness knew;*
> *So is a man's fate born.*
> *He cometh reaper of the things he sowed.*

He who would be blest, let him scatter blessings. He who would be happy, let him consider the happiness of others.

Then there is another side to this seed sowing. The farmer must scatter all his seed upon the land, and then leave it to the elements. Were he to covetously hoard his seed, he would lose both it and his produce, for his seed would perish. It perishes when he sows it, but in perishing it brings forth a great abundance. So in life, we get by giving; we grow rich by scattering. The man who says he is in possession of knowledge which he cannot give out because the world is incapable of receiving it, either does not possess such knowledge, or, if he does, will soon be deprived of it—if he is not already so deprived. To hoard is to lose; to exclusively retain is to be dispossessed.

Even the man who would increase his material wealth must be willing to part with (invest) what little capital he has, and then wait for the increase. So long as he retains his hold on his precious money, he will not only remain poor, but will be growing poorer everyday. He will, after all, lose the thing he loves, and will lose it without increase. But if he wisely lets it go; if, like the farmer, he scatters his seeds of gold, then he can faithfully wait for, and reasonably expect, the increase.

Men are asking God to give them peace and purity, and righteousness and blessedness, but are not obtaining these things; and why not? Because they are not practising them, not sowing them. I once heard a preacher pray very earnestly for forgiveness, and shortly afterwards, in the course of his sermon, he called upon his congregation to "show no mercy to the enemies of the church." Such self-delusion is pitiful, and men have yet to learn that the way to obtain peace and blessedness is to scatter peaceful and blessed thoughts, words, and deeds.

Men believe that they can sow the seeds of strife, impurity, and unbrotherliness, and then gather in a rich harvest of peace, purity and concord by merely asking for it. What more pathetic sight than to see an irritable and quarrelsome man praying for peace. Men reap that which they sow, and any man can reap all blessedness now and at once, if he will put aside selfishness, and sow broadcast the seeds of kindness, gentleness, and love.

If a man is troubled, perplexed, sorrowful, or unhappy, let him ask:

"What mental seeds have I been sowing?"

"What seeds am I sowing?"

"What have I done for others?"

"What is my attitude toward others?"

"What seeds of trouble and sorrow and unhappiness have I sown that I should thus reap these
bitter weeds?"

Let him seek within and find, and having
found, let him abandon all the seeds of self, and
sow, henceforth, only the seeds of Truth.

Let him learn of the farmer the simple truths
of wisdom.

The Reign of Law

The little party gods have had their day. The arbitrary gods, creatures of human caprice and ignorance, are falling into disrepute. Men have quarrelled over and defended them until they have grown weary of the strife, and now, everywhere, they are relinquishing and breaking up these helpless idols of their long worship.

The god of revenge, hatred and jealousy, who gloats over the downfall of his enemies; the partial god who gratifies all our narrow and selfish desires; the god who saves only the creatures of his particular special creed; the god of exclusiveness and favouritism; such were the gods (miscalled by us God) of our soul's infancy, gods base and foolish as ourselves, the fabrications of our selfish self. And we relinquished our petty gods with bitter tears and misgivings, and broke our idols with bleeding hands. But in so doing we did not lose sight of God; nay we drew nearer to the great, silent Heart of Love. Destroying the idols of self, we began to comprehend somewhat of the Power which cannot be destroyed, and entered into a wider knowledge of the God of Love, of Peace, of Joy; the God in whom revenge and partiality cannot exist; the God of light, from whose presence the darkness of fear and doubt and selfishness cannot choose but flee.

We have reached one of those epochs in the world's progress which witnesses the passing of the false gods; the gods of human selfishness and human illusion. The new-old revelation of one universal impersonal Truth has again dawned upon the world, and its searching light has carried consternation to the perishable gods who take shelter under the shadow of self.

Men have lost faith in a god who can be cajoled, who rules arbitrarily and capriciously, subverting the whole order of things to gratify the wishes of his worshippers, and are turning, with a new light in their eyes and a new joy in their hearts, to the *God of Law*.

And to Him they turn, not for personal happiness and gratification, but for knowledge, for understanding, for wisdom, for liberation from the bondage of self. And thus turning, they do not seek in vain, nor are they sent away empty and discomfited. They find within themselves the *reign of Law*, that every thought, every impulse, every act and word brings about a result in exact accordance with its own nature; that thoughts of love bring about beautiful and blissful conditions, that hateful thoughts bring about distorted and painful conditions, that thoughts and acts good and evil are weighed in the faultless balance of the Supreme Law, and receive their equal measure of blessedness on the one hand, and misery on the other. And thus finding they enter a new Path, the Path of *Obedience to the Law*. Entering that Path they no longer accuse, no longer doubt, no longer fret and despond, for they know that God is right, the universal laws are right, the cosmos is right, and that they themselves are wrong, if wrong there is, and that their salvation depends upon themselves, upon their own efforts, upon their personal acceptance of that which is good and deliberate rejection of that which is evil. No longer merely hearers, they become doers of the Word, and they acquire knowledge, they receive understanding, they grow in wisdom, and they enter into the glorious life of liberation from the bondage of self.

"The Law of the Lord is perfect, enlightening the eyes." Imperfection lies in man's ignorance, in man's blind folly. Perfection, which is knowledge of the Perfect Law, is ready for all who earnestly seek it; it belongs to the order of things; it is yours and mine now if we will only put self-seeking on one side, and adopt the life of self-obliteration.

The knowledge of Truth, with its unspeakable joy, its calmness and quiet strength, is not for those who persist in clinging to their "rights," defending their "interests," and fighting for their "opinions"; whose works are imbued with the personal "I," and who build upon the shifting sands of selfishness and egotism. It is for those who renounce these causes of strife, these sources of pain and sorrow; and they are, indeed, Children of Truth, disciples of the Master, worshippers of the most High.

The Children of Truth are in the world today; they are thinking, acting, writing, speaking; yea, even prophets are amongst us, and their influence is pervading the whole earth. An undercurrent of holy joy is gathering force in the world, so that men and women are moved with new aspirations and hopes, and even those who neither see nor hear, feel within themselves strange yearnings after a better and fuller life.

The Law reigns, and it reigns in men's hearts and lives; and they have come to understand the reign of Law who have sought out the Tabernacle of the true God by the fair pathway of unselfishness.

God does not alter for man, for this would mean that the perfect must become imperfect; man must alter for God, and this implies that the imperfect must become perfect. The Law cannot be broken for man, otherwise confusion would ensue; man must obey the Law; this is in accordance with harmony, order, justice.

There is no more painful bondage than to be at the mercy of one's inclinations; no greater liberty than utmost obedience to the Law of Being. And the Law is that the heart shall be purified, the mind regenerated, and the whole being brought in subjection to Love till self is dead and Love is all in all, for the reign of Law is the reign of Love. And Love waits for all, rejecting none. Love may be claimed and entered into now, for it is the heritage of all.

Ah, beautiful Truth! To know that now man may accept his divine heritage, and enter the Kingdom of Heaven!

Oh, pitiful error! To know that man rejects it because of love of self!

Obedience to the Law means the destruction of sin and self, and the realisation of unclouded joy and undying peace.

Clinging to one's selfish inclinations means the drawing about one's soul clouds of pain and sorrow which darken the light of Truth; the shutting out of oneself from all real blessedness; for "whatsoever a man sows that shall he also reap."

Verily the Law reigneth, and reigneth for ever, and Justice and Love are its eternal ministers.

The Supreme Justice

The material universe is maintained and preserved by the equilibrium of its forces.

The moral universe is sustained and protected by the perfect balance of its equivalents.

As in the physical world Nature abhors a vacuum, so in the spiritual world disharmony is annulled.

Underlying the disturbances and destructions of Nature, and behind the mutability of its forms, there abides the eternal and perfect mathematical symmetry; and at the heart of life, behind all its pain, uncertainty, and unrest, there abide the eternal harmony, the unbroken peace, and inviolable Justice.

Is there, then, no injustice in the universe? There is injustice, and there is not. It depends upon the kind of life and the state of consciousness from which a man looks out upon the world and judges. The man who lives in his passions sees injustice everywhere; the man who has overcome his passions, sees the operations of Justice in every department of human life. Injustice is the confused, feverish dream of passion, real enough to those who are dreaming it; Justice is the permanent reality in life, gloriously visible to those who have wakened out of the painful nightmare of self.

The Divine Order cannot be perceived until passion and self are transcended; the Faultless Justice cannot be apprehended until all sense of injury and wrong is consumed in the pure flames of all-embracing Love.

The man who thinks, "I have been slighted, I have been injured, I have been insulted, I have been treated unjustly," cannot know what Justice is; blinded by self, he cannot perceive the pure Principles of Truth, and brooding upon his wrongs, he lives in continual misery.

In the region of passion there is a ceaseless conflict of forces causing suffering to all who are involved in them. There is action and reaction, deed and consequence, cause and effect; and within and above all is the Divine Justice regulating the play of forces with the utmost mathematical accuracy, balancing cause and effect with the finest precision. But this Justice is not perceived—cannot be perceived—by those who are engaged in the conflict; before this can be done, the fierce warfare of passion must be left behind.

The world of passion is the abode of schisms, quarrellings, wars, law-suits, accusations, condemnations, impurities, weaknesses, follies, hatreds, revenges, and resentments. How can a man perceive Justice or understand Truth who is even partly involved in the fierce play of its blinding elements? As well expect a man caught in the flames of a burning building to sit down and reason out the cause of the fire.

In this realm of passion, men see injustice in the actions of others because, seeing only immediate appearances, they regard every act as standing by itself, undetached from cause and consequence. Having no knowledge of cause and effect in the moral sphere, men do not see the exacting and balancing process which is momentarily proceeding, nor do they ever regard their own actions as unjust, but only the actions of others. A boy beats a defenceless animal, then a man beats the defenceless boy for his cruelty, then a stronger man attacks the man for his cruelty to the boy. Each believes the other to be unjust and cruel, and himself to be just and humane; and doubtless most of all would the boy justify his conduct toward the animal as altogether necessary. Thus does ignorance keep alive hatred and strife; thus do men blindly inflict suffering upon themselves, living in passion and resentment, and not finding the true way in life. Hatred is met with hatred, passion with passion, strife with strife. The man who kills is himself killed; the thief who lives by depriving others is himself deprived; the beast that preys on others is hunted and killed; the accuser is accused, the condemner is condemned, the denouncer is persecuted.

> *By this the slayer's knife doth stab himself,*
> *The unjust judge has lost his own defender,*
> *The false tongue dooms its lie, the creeping thief*
> *And spoiler rob to render.*
> *Such is the Law.*

Passion, also has its active and passive sides. Fool and fraud, oppressor and slave, aggressor and retaliator, the charlatan and the superstitious, complement each other, and come together by the operation of the Law of Justice. Men unconsciously cooperate in the mutual production of affliction; "the blind lead the blind, and both fall together into the ditch." Pain, grief, sorrow, and misery are the fruits of which passion is the flower.

Where the passion-bound soul sees only injustice, the good man, he who has conquered passion, sees cause and effect, sees the Supreme Justice. It is impossible for such a man to regard himself as treated unjustly, because he has ceased to see injustice. He knows that no one can injure or cheat him, having ceased to injure or cheat himself. However passionately or ignorantly men may act toward him, it cannot possibly cause him any pain, for he knows that whatever comes to him (it may be abuse and persecution) can only come as the effect of what he himself has formerly sent out. He therefore regards all things as good, rejoices in all things, loves his enemies and blesses them that curse him, regarding them as the blind but beneficent instruments by which he is enabled to pay his moral debts to the Great Law.

The good man, having put away all resentment, retaliation, self-seeking, and egotism, has arrived at a state of equilibrium, and has thereby become identified with the Eternal and Universal Equilibrium. Having lifted himself above the blind forces of passion, he understands those forces, contemplates them with a calm penetrating insight, like the solitary dweller upon a mountain who looks down upon the conflict of the storms beneath his feet. For him, injustice has ceased, and he sees ignorance and suffering on the one hand and enlightenment and bliss on the other. He sees that not only do the fool and the slave need his sympathy, but that the fraud and the oppressor are equally in need of it, and so his compassion is extended toward all.

The Supreme Justice and the Supreme Love are one. Cause and effect cannot be avoided; consequences cannot be escaped.

While a man is given to hatred, resentment, anger and condemnation, he is subject to injustice as the dreamer to his dream, and cannot do otherwise than see injustice; but he who has overcome those fiery and binding elements, knows that unerring Justice presides over all, that in reality there is no such thing as injustice in the whole of the universe.

The Use
of Reason

We have heard it said that reason is a blind guide, and that it draws men away from Truth rather than leads them to it. If this were true, it were better to remain, or to become, unreasonable, and to persuade others so to do. We have found, however, that the diligent cultivation of the divine faculty of reason brings about calmness and mental poise, and enables one to meet cheerfully the problems and difficulties of life.

It is true there is a higher light than reason; even that of the Spirit of Truth itself, but without the aid of reason, Truth cannot be apprehended. They who refuse to trim the lamp of reason will never, whilst they so refuse, perceive the light of Truth, for the light of reason is a reflection of that Light.

Reason is a purely abstract quality, and comes midway between the animal and divine conscious-ness in man, and leads, if rightly employed, from the darkness of one to the Light of the other. It is true that reason may be enlisted in the service of the lower, self-seeking nature, but this is only a result of its partial and imperfect exercise. A fuller development of reason leads away from the self-ish nature, and ultimately allies the soul with the highest, the divine.

That spiritual Percival who, searching for the Holy Grail of the Perfect Life, is again and again

left alone,
And wearying in a land of sand and thorns,

is not so stranded because he has followed rea-son, but because he is still clinging to, and is reluc-tant to leave, some remnants of his lower nature. He who will use the light of reason as a torch to search for Truth will not be left at last in comfort-less darkness.

"Come, now, and let us reason together, saith the Lord; though your sins be as scarlet, they shall be as white as snow."

Many men and women pass through untold sufferings, and at last die in their sins, *because they refuse to reason*; because they cling to those dark delusions which even a faint glimmer of the light of reason would dispel; and all must use their reason freely, fully, and faithfully, who would exchange the scarlet robe of sin and suffering for the white garment of blamelessness and peace.

It is because we have proved and know these truths that we exhort men to

tread the middle road, whose course
Bright reason traces, and soft quiet
smooths,

for reason leads away from passion and self-ishness into the quiet ways of sweet persuasion and gentle forgiveness, and he will never be led astray, nor will he follow blind guides, who faithfully adheres to the Apostolic injunction, "Prove all things, and hold fast that which is good." They, therefore, who despise the light of reason, despise the Light of Truth.

Large numbers of people are possessed of the strange delusion that reason is somehow intimately connected with the denial of the existence of God. This is probably due to the fact that those who try to prove that there is no God usually profess to take their stand upon reason, while those who try to prove the reverse generally profess to take their stand on faith. Such argumentative combatants, however, are frequently governed more by prejudice than either reason or faith, their object being not to find Truth, but to defend and confirm a preconceived opinion.

Reason is concerned, not with ephemeral opinions, but with the established truth of things, and he who is possessed of the faculty of reason in its purity and excellence can never be enslaved by prejudice, and will put from him all preconceived opinions as worthless. He will neither attempt to prove nor disprove, but after balancing extremes and bringing together all apparent contradictions, he will carefully and dispassionately weigh and consider them, and so arrive at Truth.

Reason is, in reality, associated with all that is pure and gentle, moderate and just. It is said of a violent man that he is "unreasonable," of a kind and considerate man that he is "reasonable," and of an insane man that he has "lost his reason." Thus it is seen that the word is used, even to a great extent unconsciously, though none the less truly, in a very comprehensive sense, and though reason is not actually love and thoughtfulness and gentleness and sanity, it leads to and is intimately connected with these divine qualities, and cannot, except for purposes of analysis, be dissociated from them.

Reason represents all that is high and noble in man. It distinguishes him from the brute which blindly follows its animal inclinations, and just in the degree that man disobeys the voice of reason and follows his inclinations does he become brutish. As Milton says:

Reason in man obscured, or not obeyed,
Immediately inordinate desires
And upstart passions catch the government
From reason, and to servitude reduce
Man till then free.

The following definition of "reason" from Nuttall's Dictionary will give some idea of the comprehensiveness of the word:

The cause, ground, principle, or motive of
anything said or done; efficient cause; final cause;
the faculty of intelligence in man; especially the
faculty by which we arrive at necessary truth.

It will thus be seen that "reason" is a term, the breadth of which is almost sufficient to embrace even Truth itself, and Archbishop Trench tells us in his celebrated work On the Study of Words that the terms Reason and Word "are indeed so essentially one and the same that the Greek language has one word for them both," so that the Word of God is the Reason of God; and one of the renderings of Lao-tze's "Tao" is Reason, so that in the Chinese translation of our New Testament, St. John's Gospel runs: "In the beginning was the Tao."

To the undeveloped and uncharitable mind all words have narrow applications, but as a man enlarges his sympathies and broadens his intelligence, words become filled with rich meanings and assume comprehensive proportions. Let us therefore cease from foolish quarrelings about words, and, like reasonable beings, search for principles and practise those things which make for unity and peace.

Self-Discipline

A man does not live until he begins to discipline himself; he merely exists. Like an animal he gratifies his desires and pursues his inclinations just where they may lead him. He is happy as a beast is happy, because he is not conscious of what he is depriving himself; he suffers as the beast suffers, because he does not know the way out of suffering. He does not intelligently reflect upon life, and lives in a series of sensations, longings, and confused memories which are unrelated to any central idea or principle. A man whose inner life is so ungoverned and chaotic must necessarily manifest this confusion in the visible conditions of his outer life in the world; and though for a time, running with the stream of his desires, he may draw to himself a more or less large share of the outer necessities and comforts of life, he never achieves any real success nor accomplishes any real good, and sooner or later worldly failure and disaster are inevitable, as the direct result of the inward failure to properly adjust and regulate those mental forces which make the outer life.

Before a man accomplish anything of an enduring nature in the world he must first of all acquire some measure of success in the management of his own mind. This is as mathematical a truism as that two and two are four, for, "out of the heart are the issues of life." If a man cannot govern the forces within himself, he cannot hold a firm hand upon the outer activities which form his visible life. On the other hand, as a man succeeds, in governing himself he rises to higher and higher levels of power and usefulness and success in the world.

The only difference between the life of the beast and that of the undisciplined man is that the man has a wider variety of desires, and experiences a greater intensity of suffering. It may be said of such a man that he is dead, being truly dead to self-control, chastity, fortitude, and all the nobler qualities which constitute life. In the consciousness of such a man the crucified Christ lies entombed, awaiting that resurrection which shall revivify the mortal sufferer, and wake him up to a knowledge of the realities of his existence.

With the practice of self-discipline a man begins to live, for he then commences to rise above the inward confusion and to adjust his conduct to a steadfast centre within himself. He ceases to follow where inclination leads him, reins in the steed of his desires, and lives in accordance with the dictates of reason and wisdom. Hitherto his life has been without purpose or meaning, but now he begins to consciously mould his own destiny; he is "clothed and in his right mind."

In the process of self-discipline there are three stages namely;

Control
Purification
Relinquishment

A man begins to discipline himself by controlling those passions which have hitherto controlled him; he resists temptation and guards himself against all those tendencies to selfish gratifications which are so easy and natural, and which have formerly dominated him. He brings his appetite into subjection, and begins to eat as a reasonable and responsible being, practising moderation and thoughtfulness in the selection of his food, with the object of making his body a pure instrument through which he may live and act as becomes a man, and no longer degrading that body by pandering to gustatory pleasure. He puts a check upon his tongue, his temper, and, in fact, his every animal desire and tendency, and this he does by referring all his acts to a fixed centre within himself. It is a process of living from within outward, instead of, as formerly, from without inward. He conceives of an ideal, and, enshrining that ideal in the sacred recesses of his heart, he regulates his conduct in accordance with its exaction and demands.

There is a philosophical hypothesis that at the heart of every atom and every aggregation of atoms in the universe there is a *motionless center* which is the sustaining source of all the universal activities. Be this as it may, there is certainly in the heart of every man and woman a selfless centre without which the outer man could not be, and the ignoring of which leads to suffering and confusion. This selfless center which takes the form, in the mind, of an ideal of unselfishness and spotless purity, the attainment of which is desirable, is man's eternal refuge from the storms of passion and all the conflicting elements of his lower nature. It is the Rock of Ages, the Christ within, the divine and immortal in all men.

As a man practises self-control he approximates more and more to this inward reality, and is less and less swayed by passion and grief, pleasure and pain, and lives a steadfast and virtuous life, mani-

festing manly strength and fortitude. The restraining of the passions, however, is merely the initial
stage in self-discipline, and is immediately followed by the process of Purification. By this a man
so purifies himself as to take passion out of the
heart and mind altogether; not merely restraining
it when it rises within him, but preventing it from
rising altogether. By merely restraining his passions a man can never arrive at peace, can never
actualise his ideal; he must purify those passions.

It is in the purification of his lower nature that
a man becomes strong and God-like, standing
firmly upon the ideal centre within, and rendering all temptations powerless and ineffectual. This
purification is effected by thoughtful care, earnest
meditation, and holy aspiration; and as success is
achieved confusion of mind and life pass away,
and calmness of mind and spiritualized conduct
ensure.

True strength and power and usefulness are
born of self-purification, for the lower animal
forces are not lost, but are transmuted into intellectual and spiritual energy. The pure life (Pure
in thought and deed) is a life of conservation of
energy; the impure life (even should the impurity
not extent beyond thought) is a life of dissipation
of energy. The pure man is more capable, and
therefore more fit to succeed in his plans and to

accomplish his purposes than the impure. Where the impure man fails, the pure man will step in and be victorious, because he directs his energies with a calmer mind and a greater definiteness and strength of purpose.

With the growth in purity; all the elements which constitute a strong and virtuous manhood are developed in an increasing degree of power, and as a man brings his lower nature into subjection, and makes his passions do his bidding, just so much will he mould the outer circumstances of his life, and influence others for good.

The third stage of self-discipline, that of Relinquishment, is a process of letting the lower desires and all impure and unworthy thoughts drop out of the mind, and also refusing to give them any admittance, leaving them to perish. As a man grows purer, he perceives that all evil is powerless, unless it receives his encouragement, and so he ignores it, and lets it pass out of his life. It is by pursuing this aspect of self-discipline that a man enters into and realises the divine life, and manifests those qualities which are distinctly divine, such as wisdom, patience, non-resistance, compassion, and love. It is here, also, where a man becomes consciously immortal, rising above all the fluctuations and uncertainties of life, and living in an intelligent and unchangeable peace.

By self-discipline a man attains to every degree of virtue and holiness, and finally becomes a purified son of God, realising his oneness with the central heart of all things.

Without self-discipline a man drifts lower and lower, approximating more and more nearly to the beast, until at last he grovels, a lost creature, in the mire of his own befoulment. By self-discipline a man rises higher and higher, approximating more and more nearly to the divine, until at last he stands erect in his divine dignity, a saved soul, glorified by the radiance of his purity. Let a man discipline himself, and he will live; let a man cease to discipline himself, and he will perish. As a tree grows in beauty, health, and fruitfulness by being carefully pruned and tended, so a man grows in grace and beauty of life by cutting away all the branches of evil from his mind, and as he tends and develops the good by constant and unfailing effort.

As a man by practise acquires proficiency in his craft, so the earnest man acquires proficiency in goodness and wisdom. Men shrink from self-discipline because in its early stages it is painful and repellent, and the yielding to desire is, at first, sweet and inviting; but the end of desire is darkness and unrest, whereas the fruits of discipline are immortality and peace.

Resolution

Resolution is the directing and impelling force in individual progress. Without it no substantial work can be accomplished. Not until a man brings resolution to bear upon his life does he consciously and rapidly develop, for a life without resolution is a life without aims, and a life without aims is a drifting and unstable thing.

Resolution may of course be linked to downward tendencies, but it is more usually the companion of noble aims and lofty ideals, and I am dealing with it in this its highest use and application.

When a man makes a resolution, it means that he is dissatisfied with his condition, and is commencing to take himself in hand with a view to producing a better piece of workmanship out of the mental materials of which his character and life are composed, and in so far as he is true to his resolution he will succeed in accomplishing his purpose.

The vows of the saintly ones are holy resolutions directed toward some victory over self, and the beautiful achievements of holy men and the glorious conquests of the Divine Teachers were rendered possible and actual by the pursuit of unswerving resolution.

To arrive at the fixed determination to walk a higher path than heretofore, although it reveals the great difficulties which have to be surmounted, it yet makes possible the treading of that path, and illuminates its dark places with the golden halo of success.

The true resolution is the crisis of long thought, protracted struggle, or fervent but unsatisfied aspiration. It is no light thing, no whimsical impulse or vague desire, but a solemn and irrevocable determination not to rest nor cease from effort until the high purpose which is held in view is fully accomplished.

Half-hearted and premature resolution is no resolution at all, and is shattered at the first difficulty.

A man should be slow to form a resolution. He should searchingly examine his position and take into consideration every circumstance and difficulty connected with his decision, and should be fully prepared to meet them. He should be sure that he completely understands the nature of his resolution, that his mind is finally made up, and that he is without fear and doubt in the matter. With the mind thus prepared, the resolution that is formed will not be departed from, and by the aid of it a man will, in due time, accomplish his strong purpose.

Hasty resolutions are futile.

The mind must be fortified to endure.

Immediately the resolution to walk a higher path is made, temptation and trial begin. Men have found that no sooner have they decided to lead a truer and nobler life than they have been overwhelmed with such a torrent of new temptations and difficulties as make their position almost unendurable, and many men, because of this, relinquish their resolution.

But these temptations and trials are a necessary part of the work of regeneration upon which the man has decided and must be hailed as friends and met with courage if the resolution is to do its work. For what is the real nature of a resolution? Is it not the sudden checking of a particular stream of conduct, and the endeavour to open up an entirely new channel? Think of an engineer who decides to turn the course of a powerfully running stream or river in another direction. He must first cut his new channel, and must take every precaution to avoid failure in the carrying out of his undertaking. But when he comes to the all-important task of directing the stream into its new channel, then the flowing force, which for ages has steadily pursued its accustomed course, becomes refractory, and all the patience and care and skill of the engineer will be required for the successful completion of the work. It is even so with the man who determines to turn his course of conduct in another and higher direction. Having prepared his mind, which is the cutting of a new channel, he then proceeds to the work of redirecting his mental forces—which have hitherto flowed on uninterruptedly—into the new course. Immediately this is attempted, the arrested energy begins to assert itself in the form of powerful temptations and trials hitherto unknown and unencountered. And this is exactly as it should be; it is the law; and the same law that is in the water is in the mind. No man can improve upon the established law of things, but he can learn to understand the law instead of complaining, and wishing things were different. The man who understands all that is involved in the regeneration of his mind will "glory in tribulations," knowing that only by passing through them can he gain strength, obtain purity of heart, and arrive at peace. And as the engineer at last (perhaps after many mistakes and failures) succeeds in getting the stream to flow on peacefully in the broader and better channel, and the turbulence of the water is spent, and all dams can be removed, so the man of resolution at last succeeds in directing his thoughts and acts into the better and nobler way to which he aspires, and temptations and trials give place to steadfast strength and settled peace.

He whose life is not in harmony with his conscience and who is anxious to remedy his mind and conduct in a particular direction, let him first mature his purpose by earnest thought and self-examination, and having arrived at a final conclusion, let him frame his resolution, and having done so let him not swerve from it, let him remain true to his decision under all circumstances, and he cannot fail to achieve his good purpose; for the Great Law ever shields and protects him who, no matter how deep his sins, or how great and many his failures and mistakes, has, deep in his heart, resolved upon the finding of a better way, and every obstacle must at last give way before a matured and unshaken resolution.

The Glorious Conquest

Truth can only be apprehended by the conquest of self.

Blessedness can only be arrived at by overcoming the lower nature.

The way of Truth is barred by a man's self.

The only enemies that can actually hinder him are his own passions and delusions.

Until a man realises this, and commences to cleanse his heart, he has not found the Path which leads to knowledge and peace.

Until passion is transcended, Truth remains unknown. This is the Divine Law.

A man cannot keep his passions and have Truth as well.

Error is not slain until selfishness is dead.

The overcoming of self is no mystical theory, but a very real and practical thing.

It is a process which must be pursued daily and hourly, with unswerving faith and undaunted resolution if any measure of success is to be achieved.

The process is one of orderly growth, having its sequential stages, like the growth of a tree; and as fruit can only be produced by carefully and patiently training the tree even so the pure and satisfying fruits of holiness can only be obtained by faithfully and patiently training the mind in the growth of right thought and conduct.

There are five steps in the overcoming of passion (which includes all bad habits and particular forms of wrong-doing) which I will call:

Repression
Endurance
Elimination
Understanding
Victory

When men fail to overcome their sins, it is because they try to begin at the wrong end. They want to have the stage of Victory without passing through the previous four stages. They are in the position of a gardener who wants to produce good fruit without training and attending to his trees.

Repression consists in checking and controlling the wrong act (such as an outburst of temper, a hasty or unkind word, a selfish indulgence etc.), and not allowing it to take actual form. This is equivalent to the gardener nipping off the useless buds and branches from his tree. It is a necessary process, but a painful one. The tree bleeds while undergoing the process, and the gardener knows that it must not be taxed too severely. The heart also bleeds when it refuses to return passion for passion, when it ceases to defend and justify itself. It is the process of "mortifying the members" of which St. Paul speaks.

But this repression is only the beginning of self-conquest. When it is made an end in itself, and there is no object of finally purifying the heart, that is a stage of hypocrisy; a hiding of one's true nature, and striving to appear better in the eyes of others than one really is. In that case it is an evil, but when adopted as the first stage toward complete purification, it is good. Its practice leads to the second stage of *Endurance*, or forbearance, in which one silently endures the pain which arises in the mind when it is brought in contact with certain actions and attitudes of other minds toward one. As success is attained in this stage, the striver comes to see that all his pain actually arises in his own weaknesses, and not in the wrong attitudes of others toward him, these latter being merely the means by which his sins are brought to the surface and revealed to him. He thus gradually exonerates all others from blame in his falls and lapses of conduct, and accuses only himself, and so learns to love those who thus unconsciously reveal to him his sins and shortcomings.

Having passed through these two stages of self-crucifixion, the disciple enters the third, that of *Elimination*, in which the wrong thought which lay behind the wrong act is cast from the mind immediately it appears. At this stage, conscious strength and holy joy begin to take the place of pain, and the mind having become comparatively calm, the striver is enabled to gain a deeper insight into the complexities of his mind, and thus to understand the inception, growth, and outworking of sin. This is the stage of *Understanding*.

Perfection in understanding leads to the final conquest of self, a conquest so complete that the sin can no more rise in the mind even as a thought or impression; for when the knowledge of sin is complete; when it is known in its totality, from its inception as a seed in the mind to its ripened outgrowth as act and consequence, then it can no more be allowed a place in life, but it is abandoned for ever. Then the mind is at peace. The wrong acts of others no longer arouse wrong and pain in the mind of the disciple. He is glad and calm and wise. He is filled with Love, and blessedness abides with him. And this is *Victory*!

Contentment In Activity

The confounding of a positive spiritual virtue or principle with a negative animal vice is common amongst writers even of what is called the "Advance Thought School," and much valuable energy is frequently expended in criticising and condemning, where a little calm reasoning would have revealed a greater light, and led to the exercise of a broader charity.

The other day I came across a vigorous attack upon the teaching of "Love," wherein the writer condemned such teaching as weakly, foolish, and hypocritical. Needless to say, that which he was condemning as "Love," was merely weak sentimentality and hypocrisy.

Another writer in condemning "meekness" does not know that what he calls meekness is only cowardice, while another who attacks "chastity" as "a snare," is really confusing painful and hypocritical restraint with the virtue of chastity. And just lately I received a long letter from a correspondent who took great pains to show me that "contentment" is a vice, and is the source of innumerable evils.

That which my correspondent called "contentment" is, of course *animal indifference.* The spirit of indifference is incompatible with progress, whereas the spirit of contentment may, and does, attend the highest form of activity, the truest advancement and development. Indolence is the twin sister of indifference, but cheerful and ready action is the friend of contentment.

Contentment is a virtue which becomes lofty and spiritual in its later developments, as the mind is trained to perceive and the heart to receive the guidance, in all things, of a merciful law.

To be contented does not mean to forego effort; it means to *free effort from anxiety*; it does not mean to be satisfied with sin and ignorance and folly, but to rest happily in duty done, work accomplished.

A man may be said to be content to lead a grovelling life, to remain in sin and in debt, but such a man's true state is one of indifference to his duty, his obligations, and the just claims of his

fellow-men. He cannot truly be said to possess the
virtue of contentment; he does not experience the
pure and abiding joy which is the accompaniment
of active contentment; so far as his true nature
is concerned he is a sleeping soul, and sooner or
later will be awakened by intense suffering, having passed through which he will find that true
contentment which is the outcome of honest effort
and true living.

There are three things with which a man should
be content:

With whatever happens.

With his friendships and possessions.

With his pure thoughts.

Contented with whatever happens, he will
escape grief; with his friends and possessions, he
will avoid anxiety and wretchedness; and with his
pure thoughts, he will never go back to suffer and
grovel in impurities.

There are three things with which a man should
not be content:

With his opinions.

With his character.

With his spiritual condition.

Not content with his opinions, he will continually increase in intelligence; not content with his

character, he will ceaselessly grow in strength and virtue; and not content with his spiritual condition, he will, everyday, enter into a larger wisdom and fuller blessedness. In a word, a man should be contented, but not indifferent to his development as a responsible and spiritual being.

The truly contented man works energetically and faithfully, and accepts all results with an untroubled spirit, trusting, at first, that all is well, but afterwards, with the growth of enlightenment, *knowing* that results exactly correspond with efforts. Whatsoever material possessions come to him, come not by greed and anxiety and strife, but by right thought, wise action, and pure exertion.

The Temple of Brotherhood

Universal Brotherhood is the supreme Ideal of Humanity, and toward that Ideal the world is slowly but surely moving.

Today, as never before, numbers of earnest men and women are striving to make this Ideal tangible and real; Fraternities are springing up on every hand, and Press and Pulpit, the world over, are preaching the Brotherhood of Man.

The unselfish elements in all such efforts cannot fail to have their effect upon the race, and are with certainty urging it toward the goal of its noblest aspirations; but the ideal state has not yet manifested through any outward organisation, and societies formed for the purpose of propagating Brotherhood are continually being shattered to pieces by internal dissension.

The Brotherhood for which Humanity sighs is withheld from actuality by Humanity itself; nay, more, it is frustrated even by men who work zealously for it is a desirable possibility; and this because the purely *spiritual* nature of Brotherhood is not perceived, and the principles involved, as well as the individual course of conduct necessary to perfect unity, are not comprehended.

Brotherhood as a human organisation cannot exist so long as any degree of self-seeking reigns in the hearts of men and women who band themselves together for any purpose, as such self-seeking must eventually rend the Seamless Coat of loving unity. But although organised Brotherhood has so far largely failed, any man may realise Brotherhood in its perfection, and know it in all its beauty and completion, if he will make himself of a wise, pure, and loving spirit, removing from his mind every element of strife, and learning to practise those divine qualities without which Brotherhood is but a mere theory, opinion, or illusive dream.

For Brotherhood is at first spiritual, and its outer manifestation in the world must follow as a natural sequence.

As a spiritual reality it must be discovered by each man for himself, and in the only place where spiritual realities can be found—*within himself*, and it rests with each whether he shall choose or refuse it.

There are four chief tendencies in the human mind which are destructive of Brotherhood, and which bar the way to its comprehension, namely:

Pride
Self-love
Hatred
Condemnation

Where these are there can be no Brotherhood; in whatsoever heart these hold sway, discord rules, and Brotherhood is not realised, for these tendencies are, in their very nature, dark and selfish and always make for disruption and destruction. From these four things proceeds that serpent brood of false actions and conditions which poison the heart of man, and fill the world with suffering and sorrow.

Out of the spirit of *Pride* proceed envy, resentment, and opinionativeness. Pride envies the position, influence, or goodness of others; it thinks, "I am more deserving than this man or this woman"; it also continually finds occasion for resenting the actions of others, and says, "I have been snubbed," "I have been insulted," and thinking altogether of his own excellence, it sees no excellence in others.

From the spirit of *Self-love* proceed egotism, lust for power, and disparagement and contempt. Self-love worships the personality in which it moves; it is lost in the adoration and glorification of that "I," that "self" which has no real existence, but is a dark dream and a delusion. It desires pre-eminence over others, and thinks, "I am great," "I am more important than others"; it also disparages others, and bestows upon them contempt, seeing no beauty in them, being lost in the contemplation of its own beauty.

From the spirit of *Hatred* proceed slander, cruelty, reviling, and anger. It strives to overcome evil by adding evil to it. It says, "This man has spoken of me ill, I will speak still more ill of him and thus teach him a lesson." It mistakes cruelty for kindness, and causes its possessor to revile a reproving friend. It feeds the flames of anger with bitter and rebellious thoughts.

From the spirit of *Condemnation* proceed accusation, false pity, and false judgement. It feeds itself on the contemplation of evil, and cannot see the good. It has eyes for evil only, and finds it in almost every thing and every person. It sets up an arbitrary standard of right and wrong by which to judge others, and it thinks, "This man does not do as I would have him do, he is therefore evil, and I will denounce him." So blind is the spirit of condemnation that whilst rendering its possessor incapable of judging himself, it causes him to set himself up as the judge of all the earth.

From the four tendencies enumerated, no element of brotherliness can proceed. They are deadly mental poisons, and he who allows them to rankle in his mind, cannot apprehend the peaceful principles on which Brotherhood rests.

Then there are chiefly four divine qualities which are productive of Brotherhood; which are, as it were, the foundation stones on which it rests, namely:

Humility
Self-surrender
Love
Compassion

Wheresoever these are, there Brotherhood is active. In whatsoever heart these qualities are dominant, there Brotherhood is an established reality, for they are, in their very nature, unselfish and are filled with the revealing Light of Truth. There is no darkness in them, and where they are, so powerful is their light, that the dark tendencies cannot remain, but are dissolved and dissipated.

Out of these four qualities proceed all those angelic actions and conditions which make for unity and bring gladness to the heart of man and to the world.

From the spirit of *Humility* proceed meekness and peacefulness; from *Self-surrender* come patience, wisdom, and true judgment; from Love spring kindness, joy, and harmony; and from *Compassion* proceed gentleness and forgiveness.

He who has brought himself into harmony with these four qualities is divinely enlightened; he sees whence the actions of men proceed and whither they tend, and therefore can no longer live in the exercise of the dark tendencies. He has realised Brotherhood in its completion as freedom from malice; from envy, from bitterness, from contention, from condemnation. All men are his brothers, those who live in the dark tendencies, as well as those who live in the enlightened qualities, for he knows that when they have perceived the glory and beauty of the Light of Truth, the dark tendencies will be dispelled from their minds. He has but one attitude of mind toward all, that of good-will.

Of the four dark tendencies are born ill-will and strife; of the four divine qualities are born good-will and peace.

Living in the four tendencies a man is a strife-producer. Living in the four qualities a man is a peace-maker.

Involved in the darkness of the selfish tendencies, men believe that they can fight for peace, kill to make alive, slay injury by injuring, restore love by hatred, unity by contention, kindness by cruelty, and establish Brotherhood by erecting their own opinions (which they themselves will, in the course of time, abandon as worthless) as objects of universal adoration.

The wished-for Temple of Brotherhood will be erected in the world when its four foundation stones of Humility, Self-surrender, Love, and Compassion are firmly laid in the hearts of men, for Brotherhood consists, first of all, in the abandonment of self by the individual, and its after-effect is unity between man and man.

Theories and schemes for propagating Brotherhood are many, but Brotherhood itself is one and unchangeable and consists in the complete cessation from egotism and strife, and in practising good-will and peace; for Brotherhood is a practice and not a theory. Self-surrender and Good-will are its guardian angels, and peace is its habitation.

Where two are determined to maintain an opposing opinion, the clinging to self and ill-will are there, and Brotherhood is absent.

Where two are prepared to sympathise with each other, to see no evil in each other, to serve and not to attack each other, the Love of Truth and Good-will are there, and Brotherhood is present.

All strifes, divisions, and wars inhere in the proud, unyielding self; all peace, unity, and concord inhere in the Principles which the yielding up of self reveals.

Brotherhood is only practised and known by him whose heart is at peace with all the world.

Pleasant Pastures of Peace

He who aspires to the bettering of himself and humanity should ceaselessly strive to arrive at the exercise of that blessed attitude of mind by which he is enabled to put himself, mentally and sympathetically in the place of others, and so, instead of harshly and falsely judging them, and thereby making himself unhappy without adding to the happiness of those others, he will enter into their experience, will understand their particular frame of mind, and will feel for them and sympathise with them.

One of the great obstacles to the attainment of such an attitude of mind is, prejudice, and until this is removed it is impossible to act toward others as we would wish others to act toward us.

Prejudice is destructive of kindness, sympathy, love and true judgment, and the strength of a man's prejudice will be the measure of his harshness and unkindness toward others, for prejudice and cruelty are inseparable.

There is no rationality in prejudice, and, immediately it is aroused in a man he ceases to act as a reasonable being, and gives way to rashness, anger, and injurious excitement. He does not consider his words nor regard the feelings and liberties of those against whom his prejudices are directed. He has, for the time being, forfeited his manhood, and has descended to the level of an irrational creature.

While a man is determined to cling to his preconceived opinions, mistaking them for Truth, and refuses to consider dispassionately the position of others, he cannot escape hatred nor arrive at blessedness.

The man who strives after gentleness, who aspires to act unselfishly toward others, will put away all his passionate prejudice and petty opinions, and will gradually acquire the power of thinking and feeling for others, of understanding their particular state of ignorance or knowledge, and thereby entering fully into their hearts and lives, sympathising with them and seeing them as they are.

Such a man will not oppose himself to the prejudices of others by introducing his own, but will seek to allay prejudice by introducing sympathy and love, striving to bring out all that is good in men, encouraging the good by appealing to it, and discouraging the evil by ignoring it. He will realise the good in the unselfish efforts of others, though their outward methods may be very different from his own, and will so rid his heart of hatred, and will fit it with love and blessedness.

When a man is prone to harshly judge and condemn others, he should inquire how far he falls short himself, he should also reconsider those periods of suffering when he himself was misjudged and misunderstood, and, gathering wisdom and love from his own bitter experience, should studiously and self-sacrificingly refrain from piercing with anguish hearts that are as yet too weak to ignore, too immature and uninstructed to understand.

Sympathy is not required toward those who are purer and more enlightened than one's self, as the purer one lives above the necessity for it. In such a case reverence should be exercised, with a striving to lift one's self up to the purer level, and so enter into possession of the larger life. Nor can a man fully understand one who is wiser than himself, and before condemning, he should earnestly ask himself whether he is, after all, better than the man whom he has singled out as the object of his bitterness. If he is, let him bestow sympathy. If he is not, let him exercise reverence.

For thousands of years the sages have taught, both by precept and example, that evil is only overcome by good, yet still that lesson for the majority, remains unlearned. It is a lesson profound in its simplicity, and difficult to learn because men are blinded by the illusions of self. Men are still engaged in resenting, condemning, and fighting the evil in their own fellow-men, thereby increasing the delusion in their own hearts, and adding to the world's sum of misery and suffering. When they find out that their own resentment must be eradicated, and love put in its place, evil will perish for lack of sustenance.

With burning brain and heart of hate,
I sought my wronger, early, late,
And all the wretched night and day
My dream and thought was slay, and slay.
My better self rose uppermost,
The beast within my bosom lost

Itself in love; peace from afar
Shone o'er me radiant like a star.
I slew my wronger with a deed,
A deed of love; I made him bleed
With kindness, and I filled for years
His soul with tenderness and tears.

Dislike, resentment, and condemnation are all forms of hatred, and evil cannot cease until these are taken out of the heart.

But the obliterating of injuries from the mind is merely one of the beginnings in wisdom. There is a still higher and better way. And that way is so to purify the heart and enlighten the mind that, far from having to forget injuries, there will be none to remember. For it is only pride and self that can be injured and wounded by the actions and attitudes of others; and he who takes pride and self out of his heart can never think the thought, "I have been injured by another" or "I have been wronged by another."

From a purified heart proceeds the right comprehension of things; and from the right comprehension of things proceeds the life that is peaceful, freed from bitterness and suffering, calm and wise. He who thinks, "This man has injured me," has not perceived the Truth in life; falls short of that enlightenment which disperses the erroneous idea of evil as a thing to be hatefully resented. He who is troubled and disturbed about the sins of others is far from Truth; he who is troubled and disturbed about his own sins is very near to the Gate of Wisdom. He in whose heart the flames of resentment burn, cannot know Peace nor understand Truth; he who will banish resentment from his heart, will know and understand.

He who has taken evil out of his own heart cannot resent or resist it in others, for he is enlightened as to its origin and nature, and knows it as a manifestation of the mistakes of ignorance. With the increase of enlightenment, sin becomes impossible. He who sins, does not understand; he who understands does not sin.

The pure man maintains his tenderness of his heart toward those who ignorantly imagine they can do him harm. The wrong attitude of others toward him does not trouble him; his heart is at rest in Compassion and Love.

Blessed is he who has no wrongs to remember, no injuries to forget; in whose pure heart no hateful thought about another can take root and flourish.

Let those who aim at the right life, who believe that they love Truth, cease to passionately oppose themselves to others, and let them strive to calmly and wisely understand them, and in thus acting toward others they will be conquering themselves; and while sympathising with others, their own souls will be fed with the heavenly dews of kindness, and their hearts be strengthened and refreshed in the *Pleasant Pastures of Peace.*

The Shining Gateway

Contents

Editor's Foreword

S tudents of the works of James Allen all over the world will welcome with joy another book from his able pen. In this work we find the *Prophet of Meditation* in one of his deepest and yet most lucid expositions. How wonderfully he deals with fundamental principles! Here the reader will find no vague statement of generalities, for the writer enters with tender reverence into every detail of human experience. It is as though he came back to *The Shining Gate*, and, standing there, he reviewed all the way up which his own feet have travelled, passing over no temptation that is common to man; knowing that the obstacles that barred his ascending pathway, or the clouds that at times obscured his vision, are the common experiences of all those who have set their faces towards the heights of Blessed Vision. As we read his words now, he seems to stand and beckon to us, saying, "Come on, my fellow Pilgrims; it is straight ahead to the Shining Gateway; I have blazed the track for you." In sending forth this, another posthumous volume from his pen, we have no doubt but that it will help many and many an aspiring soul up to the heights, until at last they too stand within *The Shining Gateway.*

—Lily L. Allen
Bryngoleu,
Ilfracombe, England

The Shining Gateway of Meditation

Be watchful, fearless, faithful, patient, pure:
By earnest meditation sound the depths
Profound of life, and scale the heights sublime
Of Love and Wisdom. He who does not find
The Way of Meditation cannot reach
Emancipation and enlightenment.

The unregenerate man is subject to these three things—*desire, passion, sorrow.* He lives habitually in these conditions, and neither questions nor examines them. He regards them as his life itself, and cannot conceive of any life apart from them. Today he desires, tomorrow he indulges his passions, and the third day he grieves; by these three things (which are always found together) he is impelled, and does not know why he is so impelled; the inner forces of desire and passion arise, almost automatically, within him, and he gratifies their demands *sans* question; led on blindly by his blind desires, he falls, periodically, into the ditches of remorse and sorrow. His condition is not merely unintelligible to him, it is unperceived; for so immersed is he in the desire (or self) consciousness that he cannot step outside of it, as it were, to examine it.

To such a man the idea of rising above desire and suffering into a new life where such things do not obtain seems ridiculous. He associates all life with *the pleasurable gratification of desire*, and so, by the law of reaction, he also lives in the misery of afflictions, fluctuating ceaselessly between pleasure and pain.

When reflection dawns in the mind, there arises a sense (dim and uncertain at first) of a calmer, wiser, and loftier life; and as the stages of introspection and self-analysis are reached, this sense increases in clearness and intensity, so that by the time the first three stages are fully completed, a conviction of the reality of such a life and of the possibility of attaining it is firmly fixed in the mind. Such conviction, which consists of a steadfast belief in the supremacy of purity and goodness over desire and passion, is called *faith*. Such faith is the stay, support, and comfort of the man who, while yet in the darkness, is searching earnestly for the Light, which breaks upon him for the first time in all its dazzling splendour and ineffable majesty when he enters the Shining Gateway of Meditation. Without such faith he could not stand for a single day against the trials, failures, and difficulties which beset him continually, much less could he courageously fight and overcome them, and his final conquest and salvation would be impossible.

Upon entering the stage of meditation, faith gradually ripens into knowledge, and the new regenerate life begins to be realised in its quiet wisdom, calm beauty, and ordered strength, and day by day its joy and splendour increase.

The final conquest over sin is now assured. Lust, hatred, anger, covetousness, pride and vanity, desire for pleasure, wealth, and fame, worldly honour and power—all these have become dead things shortly to pass away for ever; there is no more life nor happiness in them; they have no part in the life of the regenerate one, who knows that he can never again go back to them, for now the "old man" of self and sin is dead, and the "new man" of Love and Purity is born within him. He has become (or becomes, as the process of meditation ripens and bears fruit) a new being, one in whom Purity, Love, Wisdom, and Peacefulness are the ruling qualities, and wherein strifes, envies, suspicions, hatreds, and jealousies cannot find lodgment. "Old things have passed away, and, behold, all things have become new"; men and things are seen in a different light, and a new universe is unveiled; there is no confusion; as out of the inner chaos of conflicting desires, passions, and sufferings the new being arises, there arises in the outer world of apparently irreconcilable conditions a new Cosmos, ordered, sequential, harmonious, ineffably glorious, faultless in equity.

Meditation is a process both of *purification* and *adjustment*. Aspiration is the purifying element, and the harmonising power resides in the intellectual train of thought involved.

When the stage of meditation is reached and entered upon, two distinct processes of spiritual transmutation are reached and entered upon, two distinct processes of spiritual transmutation begin to take place, namely:

1. Transmutation of passion
2. Transmutation of affliction

The two conditions proceed simultaneously, as they are interdependent, and act and react one upon the other. Passion and affliction, or sin and suffering, are two aspects of one thing, namely, the *self* in man, that self which is the source of all the troubles which afflict mankind. They represent *power*, but power wrongly used. Passion is a lower manifestation of a divine energy which possesses a higher use and application. Affliction is the limitation and negation of that energy, and is therefore a means of restoring harmony. It says, in effect, to the self-bound man, "Thus far shalt thou go and no farther." The man of meditation transfers the passional energy from the realm of evil (self-following) to the realm of good (self-overcoming). Today he reflects, tomorrow he overcomes his passions, and the third day he rejoices. The mind is drawn from its downward tendency, and is directed upwards. The base metal of error is transmuted into the pure gold of Truth. Lust, hatred, and selfishness disappear; and purity, love, and goodwill take their place. As the stage proceeds, the mind becomes more and more firmly fixed in the higher manifestations, and it becomes increasingly difficult for it to think and act in the lower; and just in the measure that the mind is freed from the lower, violent, and inharmonious activities, just so much is passion transmuted into power, and affliction into bliss.

This means that there is no such thing as affliction to the sinless man. When sin is put away, affliction disappears.

Selfhood is the source of suffering; Truth is the source of bliss.

When the unregenerate man is abused, slandered, misunderstood, or persecuted, it causes him intense suffering; but when these things are brought to bear on the regenerate man, there arises in him the rapture of heavenly bliss. None but he who has put away the great enemy, self, under his feet can fully enter into and understand the saying:

> ye, when men shall revile you, and persecute you, and shall say all manner of evil against you falsely, for my sake. Rejoice, and be exceeding glad.

And why does the righteous (regenerate) man rejoice under those conditions which cause such misery to the unrighteous (unregenerate) man? It is because, having overcome the evil in himself, he ceases to see evil without. To the good man all things are good, and he utilises everything for the good of the world. To him persecution is not an evil; it is a good. Having acquired insight, knowledge, and power, he, by meeting that persecution in a loving spirit, helps and uplifts his persecutors, and accelerates their spiritual progress, though they themselves know it not at the time. Thus he is filled with unspeakable bliss because he has conquered the forces of evil; because, instead of succumbing to those forces, he has learned how to use and direct them for the good and gain of mankind. He is blessed because he is at one with all men, because he is reconciled to the universe, and has brought himself into harmony with the Cosmic Order.

The following symbol will perhaps help the mind of the reader to more readily grasp what has been explained:

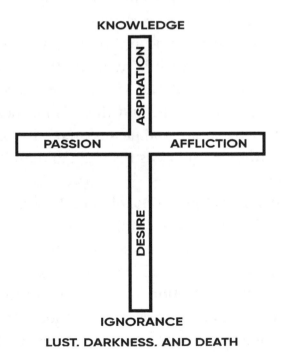

LOVE, LIGHT, AND LIFE

KNOWLEDGE

ASPIRATION

PASSION   AFFLICTION

DESIRE

IGNORANCE

LUST. DARKNESS. AND DEATH

There is at first the underworld of *lust*, *darkness*, and *death*, which is associated with *ignorance*; rooted in this is the foot of the cross—*desire*; in the body of the cross, desire branches out into two arms—the right (active or positive) arm, *passion*, being equalised and balanced by the left (passive or negative) arm of *affliction*; uniting these, and rising out of them at the head of the cross, is *aspiration*; here, wounded and bleeding, rests the thorn-crowned head of humanity; at the end of this, and right at the summit of the cross, is *knowledge*, which, while being at the apex of the self-life, is the base of the Truth-life; and above rises the heavenly world of *Love*, *Light*, and *Life*.

In this supremely beautiful world the regenerate man lives, even while living on this earth. He has reached Nirvana, the Kingdom of Heaven. He has taken up his cross, and there is no more sin and suffering; desire and passion and affliction are passed away. Harmony is restored, and all is bliss and peace.

The cross is the symbol of pain. Desire is painful, passion is painful, affliction is painful, and aspiration is painful; this is why these things are symbolised by a cross which has two pairs of conflicting poles. Affliction is the harmonising and purifying element in passion; aspiration is the harmonising and purifying element in desire. Where the one is, the other must be also. Take away the one, and the other disappears. Suffering, or affliction, is necessary to counteract passion; aspiration, or prayer, is necessary to purge away desire; but for the regenerate man all these things are ended; he has risen into a new life and a new order of things—the consciousness of purity; lacking nothing, and being at one with all things, he does not need to pray for anything; redeemed and reconciled, contented and in peace, he finds nothing in the universe to hate or fear, and his is both the duty and the power to work without ceasing for the present good and the ultimate salvation of mankind.

Temptation

I know that sorrow follows passion; know
That grief and emptiness and heartache wait
Upon all earthly joys; so am I sad;
Yet Truth must be, and being, can be found;
And though I am in sorrow, this I know—
I shall be glad when I have found the Truth.

The only external tempters of man are the *objects of sensation.* These, however, are powerless *in themselves* until they are reflected in his mind as desirable objects to possess. His only enemy, therefore, is his *coveting of the objects of sensation.* By ceasing to covet objects of sensation, temptation and the painful fighting against impure desires pass away. This ceasing to covet objects of sensation is called the *relinquishing of* desire; it is *the renunciation of the inner defilement,* by which a man ceases to be the slave of outward things, and becomes their master.

Temptation is a growth, a process more or less slow, the duration of which can be measured by the sage who has gained accurate knowledge of the nature of his thoughts and acts and the laws governing them, by virtue of having subjected himself to a long course of training in mental discipline and self-control. It has its five stages, which can be clearly defined, and their development traced with precision. But the man who is still immersed in temptation has, as yet, little or no knowledge of the nature of his thoughts and acts and the laws governing them. He has lived so long in outward things—in the objects of sensation—and has given so little time to introspection and the cleansing of his heart, that he lives in almost total ignorance of the real nature of his thoughts and acts which he thinks and commits every day. To him, temptation seems to be instantaneous, and his powerlessness to combat the sudden and, apparently, unaccountable onslaught, causes him to regard it as a *mystery*, and mystery being the mother of superstition, he may—and usually does—fall back upon some speculative belief to account for his trouble, such as the belief in an invisible Evil Being, or power, outside himself, who suddenly, and without warning, attacks and torments him. Such a superstition renders him more powerless still, for he has sufficient knowledge to understand that he cannot hope to successfully cope with a being more powerful than himself, and of whose whereabouts and tactics he is altogether unacquainted; and so he introduces other beliefs and superstitions which his dilemma seems to necessitate, until at last, in addition to all his sins and sufferings, he becomes burdened with a mass of supernatural beliefs which engross his attention, and take him farther and farther away from the real cause of his difficulty. Meantime he continues to be tempted and to fall, and must do so until by self-subjugation and self-purification he has acquired the ability to trace the relation between cause and effect in his spiritual nature, when, with purified and enlightened vision, he will see that *the moment of temptation is but the fulfilment of those impure desires which he secretly harbours in his own heart.* And, later, with a still purer heart, and when he has gained sufficient control over his wandering thoughts to be able to analyse and understand them, he will see that *the actual moment of temptation itself* has its inception, its growth, and its fruition.

What, then, are the stages in temptation? And how is the process of temptation born in the mind? How does it grow and bear its bitter fruit? The stages are five, and are as follows: 1. *Perception*; 2. *Cogitation*; 3. *Conception*; 4. *Attraction*; and 5. *Desire*.

The first stage is that in which objects of sensation are *perceived as objects*. This is pure perception, and is without sin or defilement. The second stage is that in which objects of sensation are *considered as objects of personal pleasure*. This is a brooding of the mind upon objects, with an undefined groping for pleasurable sensation, and is the beginning of defilement and sin. In the third stage objects of sensation are *conceived as objects of pleasure*. In this stage the objects are associated with certain pleasurable sensations, and these sensations are conceived and called up vividly in the mind. In the fourth stage objects of sensation are *perceived as objects of pleasure*. At this stage the pleasure as connected with the object is distinctly defined, yet there is a confusion of *pleasure* and *object*, so that the two appear as one, and a wish to possess the object arises in the mind; there is also a going out of the mind towards the object. The fifth and last stage is an intense desire, a coveting and lusting to possess the object in order to experience the pleasure and gratification which it will afford. With every repetition, in the mind, of the first four stages, this desire is added to, as fuel is added to fire, and it increases in intensity and ardour until at last the whole being is aflame with a burning passion which is blind to everything but its own immediate pleasure and gratification. And when this painful fruition of thought is reached, a man is said to be tempted. There is a still further stage of Action, which is merely the doing of the thing desired, the outworking of the sin already committed in the mind. From desire to action is but a short step.

The following table will better enable the mind of the reader to grasp the process and principle involved:

INACTION—*HOLINESS; REST*

1. Perception	Objects of Sensation *perceived* as such.
2. Cogitation	Objects of Sensation *considered* as a source of pleasure.
3. Conception	Objects of Sensation *conceived* as affording pleasure.
4. Attraction	Objects of Sensation *perceived* as pleasurable in possession.
5. Desire	Objects of Sensation *coveted* as such: *i.e.*, desired for personal delight and pleasure.

ACTION—*SIN; UNREST*

Every time a man is tempted, he passes, from *Inaction*, through all the five stages in succession, and his fall is a passing on into *Action*. The process varies greatly in duration according to the nature of the temptation and the character of the tempted; but after much yielding and many falls, the mind becomes so familiar with the transition that it passes through all the stages with such rapidity as to make the temptation appear as an instantaneous, indivisible experience.

The sage, however, never loses sight of the duration of time occupied in the process of temptation, but watches its growth and transition; and just as the scientist can measure the time occupied in the transition of sensation from the brain to the bodily extremities, or from the extremities to the brain, which, ordinarily, appears not to occupy duration, so the sage measures (though by a different method) the passage from pure perception to inflamed desire in a sudden experience of temptation.

This knowledge of the nature of temptation destroys its power, or rather its *apparent* power, for power exists in holiness only. Ignorance is at the root of all sin, and it fades away when knowledge is admitted into the mind. Just as darkness and the effects of darkness disappear when light is introduced, so sin and its effects are dispersed when knowledge of one's spiritual nature is acquired and embraced.

How, then, does the sage avoid sin and remain in peace? Knowing the nature of sinful acts—how they are the result of temptation; knowing also the nature of temptation—how it is the end and fruition of a particular train of thought, *he cuts off that train of thought at its commencement*, not allowing his mind to go out into the world of sensation, which is the world of pain and sorrow. He stands over his mind, eternally vigilant, and does not allow his thoughts to pass beyond the safe gates of *pure perception*. To him "all things are pure" because his mind is pure. He sees all objects, whether material or mental, *as they are*, and not as the pleasure-seeker sees them—as objects of personal enjoyment; nor as the tempted one sees them—as sources of evil and pain. His normal sphere, however, is that of *Inaction*, which is perfect holiness and rest. This is a position of entire indifference to considerations of pleasure and pain, regarding all things from the standpoint of *right*, and not from that of *enjoyment*. Is, then, the sage, the sinless one, deprived of all enjoyment? Is his life a dead monotony of inaction—inertia? Truly, he is delivered from all those sensory excitements which the world calls "pleasure," but which conceal, as a mask, the drawn features of pain; and, being released from the bondage of cravings and pleasures, he lives without ceasing in the divine, abiding joy which the pleasure-seeker and the wanderer in sin can neither know nor understand;

but *inaction* in this particular means inaction as regards sin; inaction in the lower animal activities which, being cut off, their energy is transferred to the higher intellectual and moral activities, releasing their power, and giving them untrammelled scope and freedom.

Thus the sage avoids sin by extracting its root within himself, not allowing it to grow into attraction, to blossom into desire, and to bear the bitter fruits of sinful actions. The unwise man, however, allows the thought of pleasure to take root in his mind, where its growth evokes sensations which are pleasant to him, and on these sensations he dwells with enjoyment, thinking in his heart, "So long as I do not commit the sinful act, I am free from sin." He does not know that his thoughts are causes the effects of which are actions, and that there is *no escape from sinful acts for him who dwells in sinful thoughts*. And so the process develops in his mind and blossoms into desire, and in the final moment of temptation (which is but the moment of opportunity brought into prominence by that desire), with the coveted object at his unreserved command, the fall of the man into sinful action is swift and certain.

Regeneration

Submit to naught but nobleness; rejoice
Like a strong athlete straining for the prize,
When thy full strength is tried; be not the slave
Of lusts and cravings and indulgences,
Of disappointments, miseries, and griefs,
Fears, doubts, and lamentations, but control
Thyself with calmness; master that in thee
Which masters others, and which heretofore
Has mastered thee; let not thy passions rule,
But rule thy passions; subjugate thyself
Till passion is transmuted into peace,
And wisdom crown thee; so shalt thou attain
And, by attaining, know.

Having considered and examined the nature of temptation in its five interdependent stages, let us now turn to the process of regeneration, and also consider its nature, so that the reader who has already received some measure of enlightenment may be still further guided in his strenuous climbing towards the Perfect Life.

The five stages in regeneration (already enumerated) are: 1. Reflection; 2. Introspection; 3. Self-analysis; 4. Meditation; and 5. Pure Perception.

The first stage in a pure and true life is that of *thoughtfulness*. The thoughtless cannot enter the right way in life. Only the reflective mind can acquire wisdom. When a man, ceasing to go after enjoyment, brings himself to a standstill in order to examine his position, and to reflect upon the condition of the world and the meaning of life, then he has entered upon the first stage of regeneration. When a man begins to think seriously, and with a deep and noble purpose in view, he has stepped out of the broad way where the thoughtless and the frivolous clutch at the bubbles of pleasure, and has entered the narrow way where the thoughtful and the wise comprehend eternal verities. Such a man's liberation from sin and suffering is already assured; for though he is, as yet, surrounded by much uncertainty, he is already realising a foretaste of the peace which awaits him; his passions, though still strong, are quieter; his mind is calmer and clearer; his intercourse with others is purer and graver; and in his moments of deepest thought he sees, as in a vision, the strength and calmness and wisdom which he knows will one day be his well-earned possessions.

Thus he passes on to the second stage.

Reflecting day by day, with ever-increasing earnestness, upon life in all its phases, he comes to perceive the passions and desires in which men are involved, and realises the sorrows which are connected with their strangely ephemeral existence. He sees the burning fevers of lusts and ambitions and cravings for pleasure, and the chilling agues of anxieties and fears, and the uncertainty of slowly approaching death, and he aspires to know the meaning of it all; is eager to find the source and cause of what seems so sorrowful and inexplicable. Recognising himself as a unit in humanity, as one involved in like passions and sorrows with all other men, he vaguely understands that somehow the secret of all life is inevitably bound up with his own existence, and so, unsatisfied with the surface theories which are based on observation only, and which still leave him subject to passions and sorrows, and the prey of anxieties and fears, he turns his thoughts inwardly upon his own mind, thinking, perchance, that the wished-for revelation of wisdom and peace awaits him there. Thus he becomes *introspective*, and so he passes on to the third stage.

When the introspective habit is fully ripened and acquired, there is called up in the mind a subtle process of inductive thought by the aid of which the innermost recesses of the man's nature, and, therefore, of all humanity, begin to unveil themselves, and yield up their secrets to the penetrating insight of the patient searcher who, unravelling now the tangled threads of thought, and tracing out the warp and woof of the web of life as it is woven in the mental processes and by the swift-flying shuttle of thought, begins, for the first time, to somewhat clearly comprehend the inner causes of human deeds, and the meaning and purpose of existence. As this process of thought is proceeded with, the desires and passions are purified away from the mind; the calmness necessary to a right perception of Truth is acquired; and gradually the fixed principles of things are presented to the comprehension, and the eternal laws of life axe coherently grasped by the understanding.

And now, quietly, and almost as imperceptibly as the soft light of dawn stealing upon the sleeping world, the neophyte, with mind purified, calmed, and controlled, passes into the fourth stage, and opens his long-sleeping eyes upon the rising light of Truth. He becomes habitually meditative, and in meditation he finds the master-key which unlocks the Door of Knowledge. It is at this advanced stage in the process of regeneration that the sinner becomes the saint, and the pupil is transformed into the master; for here the process of transmutation, hitherto slow and painful, is greatly accelerated, so that the spiritual forces formerly spent in pleasures, gratifications, passions, and afflictions are now conserved, controlled, and turned into channels of productive and reproductive thought, and so wisdom is born in the mind, and bliss, and peace.

As skill and power are acquired in meditation, the fifth and last stage is reached, where the perfect insight of the seer and the sage is evolved, so that the facts of life are grasped, and the laws and principles of things stand revealed. Here the man is altogether regenerated, is purified and perfected; all human passions are conquered, and human sorrows transcended. Here things are seen *as they are*; all the intricacies of life stand out naked in the light of Truth, and there is no more doubt and perplexity, no more sin and anguish; for he whose pure and enlightened eyes perceive the hidden causes and effects which operate infallibly in human life—he who knows how the bitter fruits of passion ripen, and where the dark waters of sorrow spring—he it is who no more sins and no more sorrows. Lo! he has come to peace.

The five stages so passed through may be thus presented:

IGNORANCE—*SIN; SUFFERING*

1. Reflection	Deep and earnest thought on the nature and meaning of life.
2. Introspection	Looking inwardly for the causes and effects which operate in life.
3. Self-analysis	Searching the springs of thought and purifying the motives in order to find the truth of life.
4. Meditation	Pure and discriminative thought on the facts and principles of life.
5. Pure Perception	Insight. Direct knowledge of the laws of life.

ENLIGHTENMENT—*PURITY; PEACE*

The whole process of regeneration may be likened to the growth of a plant. At first the small seed of *reflection* is cast into the dark soil of ignorance; then the little rootlets come forth and grope about for light and sustenance (introspection); next the strenuous *self-examination* is as the plant reaching upwards toward the light; and then the development of the bud and opening flower of *meditation*, ending at last in that pure and wise insight which is the spiritual glory of the sage, the perfect flower of enlightenment.

Thus beginning in sin and suffering, and passing through thoughtfulness, self-searching, self-purification, meditation, and insight, the seeker after the pure life and the divine wisdom reaches at last the undefiled habitation of a spotless life, and so passes beyond the dark halls of suffering, knowing the perfect Law.

Actions
and Motives

Obey the Right,
And wrong shall ne'er again assail thy peace,
Nor error hurt thee more: attune thy heart
To Purity, and thou shalt reach the Place
Where sorrow is not, and all evil ends.

It has been said that "the way to hell is paved with good intentions," and one frequently hears sin excused on the ground that it was done with a "good motive."

There are actions which are bad-in-themselves, and there are actions which are good-in-themselves, and good intentions cannot make the former good—selfish intentions cannot make the latter bad. Foremost among actions which are bad-in-themselves are those which are classified as "criminal" by all civilised communities. Thus murder, theft, adultery, libel, etc., are always bad, and it is not necessary to inquire into the motive which prompts them. Black and white remain black and white to all eternity, and are not altered by specious argumentations. A lie is eternally a lie, and no number of good intentions can turn it into a truth. If a man tell a lie with a good intention, he has none the less uttered a lie; if a man speak the truth with a selfish intention, he has none the less spoken the truth.

Besides those actions above mentioned, there are others which, while not classified by the law of the land as criminal, are yet recognised as wrong by nearly all intelligent people—actions pertaining to social and family life, and to our everyday relations with our fellowmen. Thus when a child wilfully violates its duty to its parents, the father does not stop to inquire into the motives of the child, but metes out the due correction, because the act of disobedience is *wrong-in-itself*.

The reader may here ask, "In being taught, then, to regard the motive, the condition of heart, as all important, and the act as secondary, have we been taught wrongly?" No, you have not. The motive *is* all important, for it determines the nature of the act, and here we must distinguish between *intentions* and *motives*. When people speak of good and bad motives, they nearly always mean good or bad intentions—that is, the action is done with a certain object, good or bad, in view. The motive is the deeply seated *cause* in the mind, the habitual condition of heart; the intention is the *purpose* in view. Thus an act may spring from an impure motive, yet be done with the best intention. It is possible for one to be involved in wrong motives, and yet at the same time to be so charged with good intentions as to be continually intruding himself on other people, and interfering in their business and their lives under the delusion that they "need his help."

Intentions are more or less superficial, and are largely matters of impulse, while motives are more deeply seated, and are concerned with a man's fixed moral condition. A man may do an action today with a good intention, and in a few weeks time do the same action with a bad intention; but in both instances the motive underlying the action will be the same.

In reality a wrong act cannot spring from a right motive, although it may be guided by a good intention. A man who can resort, whether habitually or under stress of temptation, to murder, theft, lying, or other actions known as bad, is in a dark, confused condition of mind, and is not capable of acting from right motives. Such acts can only spring from an impure source; and this is why the

Great Teachers rarely refer to motives, but always refer to actions. In their precepts they tell us what actions are bad and what are good, without any reference to motive, for the bad and good acts-in-themselves are the fruits of bad and good motives. "By their fruits you shall know them."

In being exhorted to "judge not," we are not taught to persuade ourselves that grapes are figs and figs grapes, but must employ our judgment in clearly distinguishing between the two; so in like manner must we distinguish with unmistakable clearness between bad actions and good actions, so as to avoid the former and embrace the latter; for only in this way can one purify his heart and render himself capable of acting from right motives. A clear perception of what is bad or good, both in ourselves and others, is not false judgment, it is wisdom. It is only when one harbours groundless suspicion about others, and reads into their actions bad and selfish intentions, that he falls into that judging against which we are warned, and which is so pernicious.

There is no need to doubt the good intentions of those about us, while, at the same time, being fully alive to a knowledge of those bad actions which were better left undone, and those good actions which were better done; taking care not to do the former, and to do the latter ourselves, thus teaching by our lives instead of accusing and condemning others. Numberless wrong actions are committed every day with good intentions; and this is why so many good purposes are frustrated and end in disappointment, because the underlying motive is impure, and the good fruit which is sought does not appear; the act is out of harmony with the good intent; the means are not adapted to the end. Bad actions bring forth bitter fruit; good actions bring forth sweet fruit.

The law runs, "Thou shalt not kill; thou shalt not steal; thou shalt not commit adultery"; not "Thou shalt not kill, steal, or commit adultery *with a bad motive.*"

Wrong actions are always accompanied with self-delusion, and the chief form which such self-delusion assumes is that of self-justification. If a man flatter himself that he can commit a sinful act, and yet be free from sin because he is prompted by a "pure motive," no limit can be set to the evil which he may commit.

It will be found that bad actions, in the majority of instances, are accompanied with good intentions. The object of the slanderer generally is to protect his fellow-men from one another. Troubled with foolish suspicions, or smarting under the thought of injury, he warns men against each other, speaking only of their bad qualities, and, in his eagerness, distorting the truth. His intention is good, namely, to protect his neighbours; but his motive is bad, namely, hatred of those whom he slanders. Such a man's good intention is frustrated by his bad action, and he at last only succeeds in separating himself from all truth-loving people.

The sore of a bad action is not cured by plastering it over with good intentions, nor is the cause of the defilement removed from the heart.

Men who are involved in bad actions cannot work from pure motives. An issue of foul water always proceeds from an impure source; and an issue of impure actions proceeds from a heart that is defiled.

It greatly simplifies life, and solves all complex problems of conduct, when certain actions are recognised as eternally bad, and others as eternally good, and the bad are for ever abandoned, and final refuge is taken in the good.

The wise and good perform good actions; and motive, act, and intention being harmoniously adjusted, their lives are powerful for good, and free from disappointment, and the good fruit of their efforts appears in due season. They do not need to defend their actions by subtle and specious arguments, not to enter into interminable metaphysical speculations concerning motives; but are content to act, and to leave their actions to bear their own fruit.

Let us not try to persuade ourselves that our good intentions will wipe out the results of our bad actions; but let us resort to the practice of good actions; for only in this way can we acquire goodness; only thus can the life be established on fixed principles, and the mind be rendered capable of comprehending, and working from, pure motives.

Morality
and Religion

The wise man
By adding thought to thought and deed to deed
In ways of good, buildeth his character.
Little by little he accomplishes
His noble ends; in quiet patience works
    Diligently.
           Daily he builds into his heart and mind
Pure thoughts, high aspirations, selfless deeds,
Until at last the edifice of Truth
Is finished, and behold! there rises and appears
The Temple of Perfection.

There is no surer indication of confusion and decadence in spiritual matters than the severance of morality from religion. "He is a highly moral man, but he is not religious"; "He is exceptionally good and virtuous, but is not at all spiritual," are common expressions on the lips of large numbers of people who thus regard religion as something quite distinct from goodness, purity, and right-living.

If religion be regarded merely and only as worship combined with adherence to a particular form of faith, then it would be correct to say, "He is a very good man, but is not religious," in some instances, just as it would be equally correct to say, "He is an immoral man, but is very religious," in other instances, for murderers, thieves, and other evil-doers are sometimes devout worshippers and zealous adherents to a creed.

Such a narrowing down of religion, however, would render much of the Sermon on the Mount superfluous, from a religious point of view, and would lead to the confounding of the *means* of religion with its *end*, the idolising of the *letter* of religion to the exclusion of the *spirit*; and this is what actually occurs when morality is severed from religion, and is regarded as something alien and distinct from it.

Religion, however, has a broader significance than this, and the most obscure creed embodies in its ritual some longing human cry for that goodness, that virtue, that morality, which many, with thoughtless judgment, divorce from religion. And is not a life of moral excellence, of good and noble character, of pure-heartedness, the very end and object of religion? Is it not the substance and spirit, of which worship and adherence to a form of faith are but the shadow and letter?

In religion, as in other things, there are the means and the end, the methods and the attainment. Worship, beliefs about God, adherence to creeds—these are some of the means; goodness, virtue, morality—these are the end. The methods are many and various, and they are embodied in countless forms of faith; but the end is one—it is moral grandeur!

Thus the moral man, far from being irreligous because he may not openly profess some form of worship, possesses the substance of religion, diffuses its spirit, has attained its end; and when the sweet kernel of religion is found and enjoyed, the shell, protective and necessary in its place, has served its purpose, and may be dispensed with.

Let not this, however, be misunderstood. The "moral" man does not refer to one who has only the outward form of morality, appearing moral in the eyes of the world, but keeping his vices secret; nor does it refer to him whose morality extends only to legal limits; nor to those who are proud of their morality—for pride is the reverse of moral—but to those who delight in purity, who are gracious, gentle, unselfish, and thoughtful, who, being good at heart, pour forth the fragrance of pure thoughts and good deeds. By the "moral" is meant the good, the pure, the noble, and the true-hearted.

A man may call himself Christian, Jew, Buddhist, Mohammedan, Hindu—or by any other name— and be immoral; but if one is pure-hearted, if he is true and noble and beautiful in character—in a word, if he is moral—then he is an inhabitant of the "Holy City" in which there is "no temple"; he is, by example and influence, a regenerator of mankind; he is one of the company of the Children of Light.

Memory,
Repetition,
and Habit

I shall gain,
By purity and strong self-mastery,
The awakened vision that doth set men free
From painful slumber and the night of grief.

When a particular combination of words has been repeated a number of times, it is said to have been committed to memory—that is, it can then be repeated without visual reference to the words themselves, and without pause or effort; indeed, the words have then a tendency to repeat themselves in the mind, and sometimes people are troubled with the ringing of a refrain, or the repetition of a sentence in the mind, which they find it very difficult to get rid of and forget.

There is a sense in which the whole of life is a process of committing to memory. At first there is *act*, from act springs *experience*, from experience arises *recollection*, from recollection *repetition*, and from repetition is formed *habit*; hence proceeds impulse, faculty, character, individualised existence.

Life is a repetition of the same things over again. There is very little difference between the days and years in the life of a man; one is almost entirely a repetition of the other. Every being is an accumulation of experiences gathered, learnt, and woven into the life by a ceaseless series of repetitions extending over an incalculable number of lives which thread their way through eons of time.

The life of a man, from the germ-cell to maturity, is a repetition, in synthesis, of the entire process of evolution. There is a cosmic memory at the root of all growth and progress, which is an informing and sustaining principle in the process of evolution.

The sensuous memory of man is fickle and ephemeral, but the supersensuous memory which is inherent in all matter, building up forms and faculty, is infallible in its reproduction of experiences.

Life is ceaseless reiteration. Nature ever travels over old and familiar ground. Man is daily repeating that which he has learnt, though the schools of experience in which the lessons were acquired may be long forgotten; but the acquired habit is not forgotten; it is carried forward and continues to act. The unconscious and automatic ease which marks the play of faculty is not the ready-made mechanism of an arbitrary creator; it is *skill acquired by practice*; it is the consummation of millions of repetitions of the same thought and act.

Thoughts and deeds long persisted in become at last spontaneous impulses.

It is a profound truth that "there is nothing new under the sun." It is possible and highly probable that, in the round of eternity, even all our modern inventions and mechanical marvels have been produced innumerable times on this or other worlds. In this world, new combinations of matter appear from time to time, but are they new in the universe? Who dare say that, in the mind which overarches eternity, the cosmic memory is not reproducing things long since fashioned out of itself?

Nothing can be added to, or taken from, the universe. Its matter can neither be increased nor decreased. Chemical combinations of matter vary, but matter itself cannot vary. Life likewise does not change. In the forms of life there is continuous flux, but in the principle of life there is no increase or diminution. Forms come forth only to retreat and disappear; but that which disappears is not lost; the memory of it is retained, and it continues to be repeated. Eternal disintegration is balanced by eternal restitution.

The mind of man is not separate from the Eternal Mind; in its daily repetitions is indelibly written the record of all its past. *Character is an accumulation of deeds.* Each man is the last reckoning in the long sum of evolution, and there is no falsification of the account. The mind continues to automatically perform the habit which encloses a million repetitions of the same deed. Compared with this ineffaceable, unconscious memory, the memory of three score years and ten is as a fading vapour to an Egyptian Pyramid. The tendencies, impulses, and habits of which a man is a victim are the repetitions of his accumulated deeds. They enfold the destiny which he has wrought. The grace, goodness, and genius which a man exhibits without conscious effort are the fruits of the accumulated labours of his mind. He repeats with ease that which was learned by painful labour. The wise man sees a reflection of himself in the fate which overtakes him.

Life flows in channels. Every man is in a rut. Men tell their fellows to "get out of their ruts," but they themselves are in ruts of another kind. The flow of law, of nature, cannot be avoided, but it can be utilised. We cannot avoid ruts, but we can avoid bad ones; we can follow along good ones.

In their training and education, the children of today are strictly Confined to ways which are worn by the feet of a thousand generations. In his fixed habits and characteristics, the man of today is reviving the actions of a thousand lives.

It is true that men are bound; but it is equally true that they can unbind. The law by which a man becomes the sorrowful victim of his own wrong deeds is a blessed, and not a cursed, law; for by the same law he can become the instrument of all that is good. Habits chain a man, but he himself forged the links. He whose inner eye has opened to perceive the law does not complain. The bondage of evil is a heavy slavery, but the bondage of good is a blessed service.

The will of man is powerless to alter the law of life, but it is powerful to obey it. The Great Law makes for good; it puts a heavy penalty on evil. Man can break his chains, and shake himself free; and when he enters earnestly upon the work of self-liberation, all the universe will be with him in his labour. Repetition and habit he cannot avoid, but he can set going repetitions that are harmonious; he can form habits that will crystallise into pure and noble characteristics.

In the self-built archives of the mind are stored away the entire records of man's evolution. Man is an epitomised history of the world. In his outbursts of rage we hear again the roar of the lion in the forest; in his selfish schemings to secure his coveted ends we see the tiger stalking its prey; his lusts, revenges, hatreds, and fears are the instinct born of primeval experiences. The universe does not forget; life remembers and restores.

Between the sensuous and the supersensuous worlds is the Lethean stream, the river of forgetfulness. Only he who has passed into the supersensuous world—the world of pure goodness—remembers with the Memory of Life which transcends a million deaths. Only he whose will obeys the Universal Will, whose heart is in harmony with the Cosmic Order, receives the vision which pierces through the vale of time and matter, and sees the before and the beyond.

Man quickly forgets, and it is well that he forgets; the universe remembers and records. The repetition of an evil deed is its own retribution; the repetition of a good deed is its own reward. The deepest punishment of evil is evil; the highest reward of good is good. When a deed is done, it is not ended; it is but begun; it remains with the doer—to curse him, if evil; to bless him, if good. Deeds accumulate by repetition, and they remain as character, and in character is both curse and blessing.

Suffering inheres in the discordant repetition of evil; bliss inheres in the rhythmic repetitions of good. Seeing that we cannot escape the law of repetition, let us choose to do those things which are good; and as one establishes habits of purity, the divine memory will be awakened within him.

Words
and Wisdom

I would find
Where Wisdom is, where Peace abides, where Truth,
Majestic, changeless, and eternal, stands
Untouched by the illusions of the world;
For surely there is Knowledge, Truth, and Peace
For him who seeks.

Thoughts, words, acts—these combine to make up the entire life of every individual. Words and acts are thoughts expressed. We think in words. In the process of thinking, words are stored up in the consciousness, where they await expression and use as occasion may call them forth.

Words fit the mind which received them; they are the tally of the intellect which uses them. The meaner the mind, the more meagre is the vocabulary. A limited and a capacious intellect alike expresses itself through a limited and an extensive use of words. A great mind expresses itself by the vehicle of flowing and noble language.

Words stand for conceptions. Conceptions are embodied in words. At the moment that a conception is formed in the mind, its corresponding word arises in the thought. Conceptions and words cannot be hidden away indefinitely. Sooner or later they will come forth into the outer world of expression. The matter of the universe is in ceaseless circulation. Its hidden things are continuously coming forth into open and visible life. Likewise the mental operations of men are ever in active circulation, and their hidden thoughts are daily expressing themselves in words and acts. The words and actions of every man are determined by the thoughts in which he habitually dwells.

Speech is audible thought. A man reveals himself through his speech. Whether he is pure or impure, foolish or wise, he makes his inner condition known through his speech. The foolish man is known by the way in which he talks; the wise man is known by the purity, gravity, and excellence of his speech. "He who would gain a knowledge of men," says Confucius, "must first learn to understand the meaning of words."

All wise men, saints, and great teachers have declared that the first step in wisdom is to control the tongue. The disciple of speech is a mental disciple. When a man controls his tongue, he controls his mind; when he purifies his speech, he purifies his mind. Speech and mind cannot be separated. They are two aspects of character.

A man may read Scripture, study religions, and practise mystical arts; but if he allows his tongue to run loosely, he will be as foolish at the end of all his labours as he was at the beginning.

A man may not read Scripture, nor study religions, nor practise ascetic arts; but if he controls his tongue, and studies how to speak wisely and well, he will become wise.

Wisdom is perceived in the words which are its expression. We speak of certain men—of Shakespeare for instance—as being wise. We never saw Shakespeare, and we know very little of his life; how, then, do we know he was wise? By his words only. Where there are wise words, we know there is a wise mind. A foolish man may, like a parrot, *repeat* wise words, but a wise man *frames* wise sentences; his wisdom is shown in originally expressed language.

Why do men speak of words as being bad or good, degrading or inspiring, low or lofty, weak or strong? Is it not because they unconsciously recognise that words cannot be dissociated from thoughts? Why do pure-minded people avoid a man who habitually uses impure language? Is it not because they know that such words proceed from an unclean mind?

It is impossible for any being to give utterance to words which are not already lodged in his mind in the form of thought. The impure mind cannot speak pure words; the pure mind cannot speak impure words. The ignorant cannot speak learnedly, nor the learned ignorantly. The foolish man cannot speak wisely, nor the wise foolishly.

Altered speech follows an altered mind. When a man turns from evil to good, his conversation becomes cleansed. As a man increases in wisdom, he watches, modifies, and perfects his speech.

If the foolish and the wise are known by their words, what, then, is the speech of folly, and what the language of wisdom?

A man is foolish:

If he talks aimlessly and incoherently.
If he engages in impure conversations
If he utters falsehood.
If he speaks ill of the absent, and carries about
    evil reports concerning others.
If he frames flattering words.
If he utters violent and abusive words.
If his speech is irreverent, and his words are
    directed against the great and good.
If he speaks in praise of himself.

A man is wise:

If he talks with purpose and intelligence.
If his conversation is chaste.
If he utters words of sincerity and truth.
If he speaks well of, and in defence of, the absent.
If he speaks words of virtuous reproof.
If his speech is gentle and kindly.
If he talks reverently of the great and good.
If he speaks in praise of others.

We are all, now and always, justified and condemned by our words. The law of Truth is not held in abeyance, and every day is judgment day. For "every idle word" which one speaks he is at once "called to account" in an immediate and certain loss of happiness and influence. By the words which we habitually utter we publish to the universe the degree of our intelligence and the standard of our morality, and receive back through them the judgment of the world. The fool thinks he is harshly judged and badly treated by others, not knowing that his real scourge is his own ungoverned tongue.

To control the tongue, to discipline the speech, to strive for the use of purer and gentler words— this is a very lowly thing, and one that is much despised; but it cannot be neglected by him who eagerly aspires to walk the way of wisdom.

Truth Made Manifest

Upon the lofty Summits of the Truth,
Where clouds and darkness are not, and
    where rests
Eternal Splendour; there, abiding Joy
Awaits thy coming.
Be watchful, fearless, faithful, patient, pure:
By earnest meditation sound the depths
Profound of life, and scale the heights sublime
Of Love and Wisdom.

Truth is rendered visible through the media of deeds. It is something seen and not heard. Words do not contain the Truth; they only symbolise it. Good deeds are the only vessels which contain Truth.

It has been frequently said that *being* must precede *doing*. Being always does precede doing; but being and doing cannot be arbitrarily separated. A man's deeds are the expression of himself. Acts are the language of Reality. If a man's inner being is allied to Truth, his deeds will speak it forth; if with error, his deeds will make manifest that error.

No man can hide what he is. He must necessarily act, and every time he acts he reveals himself.

In the light of Reality no man can deceive humanity or the universe; but he can deceive himself.

Deeds of purity, love, gentleness, patience, humility, compassion, and wisdom are Truth made manifest. These qualities cannot be contained between the covers of a book, but only the words which refer to them; they are Life.

Deeds of impurity, hatred, anger, pride, vanity, and folly are error making itself known. A man's deeds are the publication of himself to the world.

Truth cannot be comprehended through reading, but only by correcting and converting one's self. Precepts are aids to the acquirement of wisdom, but wisdom is acquired only by practice.

If a man would know what measure of Truth he possesses, he should ask himself, "What am I? What are my deeds?"

Men dispute about words, thinking that Truth is heard and read. Truth is neither heard nor read; it is *seen*.

Good deeds are the visible embodiments of Truth; they are messengers of Knowledge; angels of Wisdom; but the eye of error is dark, and cannot see them.

Spiritual Humility

Who would be the companion of the wise,
And know the Cosmic Splendour; he must stoop
Who seeks to stand; must fall who fain would rise;
Must know the low, ascending to the high;
He who would know the Great must not disdain
To diligently wait upon the small:
He wisdom finds who finds humility.

Throughout the Sacred Scriptures of all religions there runs, like a silver thread, the teaching of Humility. Not only all the Scriptures, but the sages of all time have declared that only through the portal of humility is it possible for man to enter into the possession of the Life of Truth; and as that life is entirely of a Spiritual Nature, so the humility that leads to it is purely and absolutely spiritual; and being such, it can never be materialised, can never be embodied in a dogma, or laid down as a formula. It is not an outward thing, nor does it consist of that practice of self-abasement that has usurped its name.

But priests have taught, and many have been led to believe, that self-depreciation is true humility, while in reality it is its extreme antithesis. Self-depreciation is self-degradation; nay, it is even a sort of self-destruction, it is spiritual suicide. The man who believes that all his righteousness is as filthy rags, that there is no good thing in him, and that he can never rise by any effort of his own, is, by that very attitude of his mind, rendering himself impotent; he is strangling the Spirit; he is undermining and disintegrating all that is highest and noblest in his character. Instead of building up his character he is engaged in despoiling it, "As a man thinketh in his heart, so is he"; what our thoughts are, such are our characters. We are in reality beings composed of thoughts; thoughts are the bricks which we are continually laying down in the building of our souls. If we put a large percentage of rotten bricks into the building, we shall build but a miserable hovel, and every self-depreciating thought is a brick that is already crumbling. It will be found to be a rule marvellously accurate in its application that those who continually live in this attitude of self-depreciation are throughout life, or, at any rate, until they strike a nobler attitude, wretched failures. I can bring to my mind many such men that I have known. How can it be otherwise? How can a man who has no faith in himself ever win the confidence of others, or accomplish anything worthy? Moreover, such a man has not, cannot possibly have, any faith in human nature; despising himself, he despises all; and as a result, by the unerring law of cause and effect, all men despise him. Yet it is a strange fact that the men who maintain this faith-destroying attitude of mind invariably profess to have the greatest faith in God; yea, look upon it as an infallible witness to their superior spiritual faith. But I ask this question, Does not true faith, like true charity, begin at home? In the growth of the soul faith in one's self comes first, next faith in human nature, and finally faith in God. That faith which professes to have the latter to the exclusion of the two former is false faith, the outcome of false humility.

Another kind of false humility is that of *personal abasement* to an individual or to established authority. This is humility materialised or subverted. It is the worship of Dagon, the bowing of the knee to Baal, the slavish adoration of the Golden Calf. No man can persist in it without undermining his character, and ultimately dissipating his spiritual and mental energies. Humility to man or to any temporal authority is degrading and slavish; humility to the Most High is grandly beautiful.

Spiritual humility is closely allied to faith, and the more there is of humility the more there is of faith. It is the key-note of all real greatness. In proof of this I have only to refer to the great sages, saints, and reformers of all time. The greatest of them are those who had the greatest share of spiritual humility. True humility, as distinguished from false, has a strengthening power, an upbuilding force. It inspires and invigorates the soul, spurring it to greater and ever greater endeavour.

Of what, then, does this humility consist? Is it the bending of the knee to ask personal favours of Deity? Is it the blind petitioning of God to accomplish for us our petty and narrow designs? Nay, these are its counterfeits. True humility is far above and beyond all this. It is the deepest and holiest aspiration of the human heart, where deep within, hidden from all sacrilegious gaze, it works, a silent mighty power, purifying, transforming, the man of flesh and self; entering its solitary grandeur, the alienated soul returns to the footstool of its God, and bathes, in blissful rapture, in the light of His all-embracing Love. It is a state that can only be entered into by rising above *one's lower self.* It is in fact the submergence of the self in the *non-self;* the submission of passion and intellect to the Supreme; it is the attitude of a human soul adoring its highest conceptions.

Such humility takes its possessor above all that is mean and poor in his nature, into the very presence of God, making him calm, strong, noble, self-reliant, and Godlike. It is the Wine of Life to all aspiring souls. The soul that has not felt its power is dead.

It may sound like a paradox, but it is nevertheless true, that the more a man has of humility the more he has of *independence*. But the seeming paradox will be made clear if we think for a moment of the lives of such teachers of humility as Jesus, Buddha, Confucius, Socrates, Jacob Boehme, George Fox, and indeed of all the great religious reformers. These men walked erect, because, yielding themselves up to the simplicity of humility, they walked with God.

The humility that causes a man to go, metaphorically speaking, on all fours is spurious, and is as debasing and destructive as the real humility is elevating and strengthening. Why should we go amongst our fellows like cringing, fearful beasts, calling ourselves miserable sinners? Shall we ever rise above sin by so doing? Is it possible to rise by ceaselessly contemplating our absolute unworthiness?

No, we can only rise by continually contemplating the Highest. There may be much that is unworthy in a man's heart, but there is also a sacredness, a dignity, a divinity about it; let us dwell upon that. Let us continually contemplate the goodness, the purity, and the essential beauty of human nature. Let us ceaselessly search for the Divinity in our own souls, and, finding it through the door of humility, we shall then recognise the invisible God in all men. By so doing, we rise above the binding limitations of our selfish desires, and enter the larger, healthier, holier life of Love.

Spiritual Strength

All things are holy to the holy mind,
All uses are legitimate and pure,
All occupations blest and sanctified,
And every day a Sabbath.

A clear and firm head must precede and accompany a clean and gentle heart. Without the first the second is impossible, for the qualities of purity and gentleness can only be reached through a clear perception of right and wrong, and by the exercise of an irresistible will. The strength of a powerful animal, or of that animal force in man which enables him to gain the victory over others by attack and resistance, is weakness compared with that quiet, patient, invincible will by which a man overcomes himself, and tames to obedience, and trains to the service of holy purposes, the savage passions of his nature.

Every dog can bark and fight, and every fool-ish man can rail, abuse, fence with hard words, and give way to fits of bad temper; these things are easy and natural to him, and require no effort and no strength. But the wise man puts away all such follies, and trains himself in self-control—trains himself to act unerringly from fixed principles, and not from the fleeting impulses of an unstable nature.

He who succeeds in so training himself is able to train others, in a small degree by precept, but largely and chiefly by practice or example, for it is pre-eminently the prerogative of the wise to teach by their actions. The mockeries of Herod, the accu-sations of the people, and the fanatical persecu-tions of the priests all failed to draw from Jesus the word of complaint, bitterness, or self-defence. Such sublime acts of silence and self-control continue to reach, for ages, both individuals and nations, with far greater power and effect than all the words and books uttered and written by the world's vast army of priests and learned commentators.

To retaliate and fight belongs to the animal in man as it belongs to the beast of the forest; but to refuse to be swayed from the practice of a divine principle by any external pressure—to stand firm and unalterable in goodness and truth alike amid blame and praise—this belongs to the divine in man and in the universe.

To alter one's conduct in order to please others, or to avoid their censure or misunderstanding can never lead to spiritual strength.

That divine kindness which always accompanies spiritual understanding and strength is something very different from merely saying pleasant words—for pleasant words are not always true words—but consists in doing *what is best for the eternal welfare of the other person or persons.*

The weak father, who is unfit to train children, only considers how he can escape trouble with his children, and so he slurs over their acts of disobedience and selfishness, and tries to please them. But the strong father, who considers the future character and welfare of his children, knows how and when to administer a severe reproof, fully understanding that the few minutes' pain caused by his rebuke may save his child from years of suffering as a result of loose living which is fostered by parental neglect. The strong, kind, unselfish father, whose care is for his children's good, and not for his own immediate comfort, knows not only how to be tender in affection, but tender in discipline, knows how to stretch out the strong and (to the child at the time) severe arm of restraint to save his little ones when they would ignorantly wander away in wrong paths.

So the man of spiritual strength cannot be merely a weak framer of smooth words, but a doer of right actions, an utterer of words that are vital and true, and, therefore, eternally kind.

The spiritually weak man shrinks from right when it is brought (as by its nature it must be brought) in opposition to his desires, and he embraces sin because it is pleasant. The spiritually strong man shrinks from sin, more especially when it is presented to him in a pleasant garb, and embraces right, even though by so doing he will bring upon himself the odium of those who are ignorant of divine principles and their beneficent application.

The man of spiritual understanding is as unbending as a bar of steel where right is concerned, knowing that right alone is good; he is as unresisting as water where self is concerned, knowing that self alone is evil. Acting from imperishable principles and not from the fleeting desires of self, his actions partake of the imperishable nature of the principles from which they spring, and continue to afford instruction and inspiration through unnumbered generations.

It is always the portion of one who so acts to be misunderstood. The majority live in their desires and impulses, following them blindly as they are brought into operation by external stimuli, and do not understand what is meant by acting dispassionately from right and fixed principles, with entire freedom from self-interest. Such will necessarily misunderstand and misjudge the right-doer, regarding him as cold and cruel in his unbending adherence to right, or as weak and cowardly in his quiet refusal to passionately defend himself. He will, therefore, "be accused of many things"; but this will not cause him any suffering, nor will he be troubled or disturbed thereby, for the truth which he practises is a source of perpetual joy, and he will be at rest in the knowledge that there are those who will understand and follow, that he is working for the ultimate good even of his accusers, and that, by manifesting the truth in his daily actions, he is in the company of those divinely strong ones who are leading the world into ways of quietness and peace.

About the Author

James Allen was one of the pioneering figures of the self-help movement and modern inspirational thought. A philosophical writer and poet, he is best known for his book *As a Man Thinketh*. Writing about complex subjects such as faith, destiny, love, patience, and religion, he had the unique ability to explain them in a way that is simple and easy to comprehend. He often wrote about cause and effect, as well as overcoming sadness, sorrow and grief.

Allen was born in 1864 in Leicester, England into a working-class family. His father travelled alone to America to find work, but was murdered within days of arriving. With the family now facing economic disaster, Allen, at age 15, was forced to leave school and find work to support them.

During stints as a private secretary and stationer, he found that he could showcase his spiritual and social interests in journalism by writing for the magazine *The Herald of the Golden Age.*

In 1901, when he was 37, Allen published his first book, *From Poverty to Power.* In 1902 he began to publish his own spiritual magazine, *The Light of Reason* (which would be retitled *The Epoch* after his death). Each issue contained announcements, an editorial written by Allen on a different subject each month, and many articles, poems, and quotes written by popular authors of the day and even local, unheard of authors.

His third and most famous book *As a Man Thinketh* was published in 1903. The book's minor popularity enabled him to quit his secretarial work and pursue his writing and editing career full time. He wrote 19 books in all, publishing at least one per year while continuing to publish his magazine, until his death. Allen wrote when he had a message—one that he had lived out in his own life and knew that it was good.

In 1905, Allen organized his magazine subscribers into groups (called "The Brotherhood") that would meet regularly and reported on their meetings each month in the magazine. Allen and his wife, Lily Louisa Oram, whom he had married in 1895, would often travel to these group meetings to give speeches and read articles. Some of Allen's favorite writings, and those he quoted often, include the works of Shakespeare, Milton, Emerson, the Bible, Buddha, Whitman, Trine, and Lao-Tze.

Allen died in 1912 at the age of 47. Following his death, Lily, with the help of their daughter, Nora took over the editing of *The Light of Reason*, now under the name *The Epoch*. Lily continued to publish the magazine until her failing eyesight prevented her from doing so. Lily's life was devoted to spreading the works of her husband until her death at age 84.

CPSIA information can be obtained
at www.ICGtesting.com
Printed in the USA
JSHW030001140720
6663JS00001B/55

9 781722 503512